AS Maths
OCR Core 2

AS level maths is seriously tricky — no question about that.

We've done everything we can to make things easier for you.
We've scrutinised past paper questions and we've gone through the syllabuses with a
fine-toothed comb. So we've found out exactly what you need to know, then
explained it simply and clearly.

We've stuck in as many helpful hints as you could possibly want
— then we even tried to put some funny bits in to keep you awake.

We've done our bit — the rest is up to you.

Contents

P1 — PRACTICE EXAM 1

P1 — PRACTICE EXAM 2

This book covers the Core 2 module of the OCR specification.

Published by Coordination Group Publications Ltd.

Contributors:
Charley Darbishire
Simon Little
Andy Park
Glenn Rogers
Claire Thompson

And:
Iain Nash

Updated by:
Alison Chisolm
Dominic Hall
Tim Major
Kate Manson
Sam Norman
Alan Rix
Claire Thompson
Julie Wakeling

ISBN: 1-84146-766-9

Groovy website: www.cgpbooks.co.uk

Jolly bits of clipart from CorelDRAW
With thanks to Colin Wells and Frances Knight for the proofreading.

Printed by Elanders Hindson, Newcastle upon Tyne.

Algebraic Division

Algebraic division is one of those things that you have to learn when you do AS maths. You'll probably never use it again once you've done your Exam, but hey ho... such is life.

Do **Polynomial Division** by means of **Subtraction**

$$(2x^3 - 3x^2 - 3x + 7) \div (x - 2) = ?$$

The trick with this is to see how many times you can <u>subtract</u> $(x - 2)$ from $2x^3 - 3x^2 - 3x + 7$.
The idea is to keep <u>subtracting</u> lumps of $(x - 2)$ until you've got rid of all the <u>powers of x</u>.

Do the subtracting in **Stages**

At each stage, always try to get rid of the <u>highest</u> power of x.
Then start again with whatever you've got left.

① Start with $2x^3 - 3x^2 - 3x + 7$, and <u>subtract</u> $2x^2$ lots of $(x - 2)$ to get rid of the x^3 term.

$$(2x^3 - 3x^2 - 3x + 7) - 2x^2(x - 2)$$
$$(2x^3 - 3x^2 - 3x + 7) - 2x^3 + 4x^2$$
$$= x^2 - 3x + 7$$

$2x^3 \div x = 2x^2$

This is what's left — so now you have to get rid of the $\underline{x^2}$ term.

② Now <u>start again</u> with $x^2 - 3x + 7$.
The highest power of x is the x^2 term.
So <u>subtract</u> x lots of $(x - 2)$ to get rid of that.

$$(x^2 - 3x + 7) - x(x - 2)$$
$$(x^2 - 3x + 7) - x^2 + 2x$$
$$= -x + 7$$

Now start again with this — and get rid of the $\underline{x}$ term.

③ All that's left now is $-x + 7$.
Get rid of the $-x$ by <u>subtracting</u> -1 times $(x - 2)$.

$$(-x + 7) - (-1(x - 2))$$
$$(-x + 7) + x - 2$$
$$= 5$$

There are no more powers of x to get rid of — so <u>stop here</u>.

The <u>remainder's</u> 5.

Interpreting the results...

Time to work out exactly what all that <u>meant</u>.

Started with: $2x^3 - 3x^2 - 3x + 7$

Subtracted: $2x^2(x - 2) + x(x - 2) - 1(x - 2)$
$$= (x - 2)(2x^2 + x - 1)$$

Remainder: $= 5$

So... $2x^3 - 3x^2 - 3x + 7 = (x - 2)(2x^2 + x - 1) + 5$

or... $\dfrac{2x^3 - 3x^2 - 3x + 7}{(x - 2)} = 2x^2 + x - 1$ with remainder 5.

Algebraic Division

$$(ax^3 + bx^2 + cx + d) \div (x - k) = ?$$

1) <u>SUBTRACT</u> a multiple of $(x - k)$ to get rid of the highest power of x.

2) <u>REPEAT</u> step 1 until you've got rid of all the powers of x.

3) <u>WORK OUT</u> how many lumps of $(x - k)$, you've subtracted, and the <u>REMAINDER</u>.

The Remainder and Factor Theorems

The Remainder Theorem's easy, but it's not as useful as its little brother — the Factor Theorem... but make sure you learn them both 'cos you're bound to be asked to use them.

The **Remainder Theorem** is an easy way to work out **Remainders**

When you divide $f(x)$ by $(x - a)$, the remainder is $f(a)$.

So in the example on the page 1, you could have worked out the remainder dead easily.

1) $f(x) = 2x^3 - 3x^2 - 3x + 7$.
2) You're dividing by $(x - 2)$, so $a = 2$.
3) So the remainder must be $f(2) = (2 \times 8) - (3 \times 4) - (3 \times 2) + 7 = 5$.

Careful now... when you're dividing by something like $(x + 7)$, a is negative — so here, $a = -7$.

The **Factor Theorem** is just the Remainder Theorem with a **Zero Remainder**

If you get a remainder of zero when you divide f(x) by (x – a), then (x – a) must be a factor. That's the Factor Theorem.

> ### The Factor Theorem:
> If f(x) is a polynomial, and f(a) = 0, then (x – a) is a factor of f(x).
>
> In other words: If you know the roots, you also know the factors — and vice versa.

Example: Show that $(2x + 1)$ is a factor of $f(x) = 2x^3 - 3x^2 + 4x + 3$

The question's giving you a big hint here. Notice that $2x + 1 = 0$ when $x = -\frac{1}{2}$. So plug this value of x into $f(x)$. If you show that $f(-\frac{1}{2}) = 0$, then the factor theorem says that $(x + \frac{1}{2})$ is a factor — which means that $2 \times (x + \frac{1}{2}) = (2x + 1)$ is also a factor.

$$f(x) = 2x^3 - 3x^2 + 4x + 3 \quad \text{and so} \quad f\left(-\frac{1}{2}\right) = 2 \times \left(-\frac{1}{8}\right) - 3 \times \frac{1}{4} + 4 \times \left(-\frac{1}{2}\right) + 3 = 0$$

So, by the factor theorem, $(x + \frac{1}{2})$ is a factor of $f(x)$, and so $(2x + 1)$ is also a factor.

(x – 1) is a Factor if the coefficients Add Up To 0

This is a useful thing to remember.
It works for all polynomials — no exceptions.
It could save a fair whack of time in the exam.

Example: Factorise the polynomial $f(x) = 6x^2 - 7x + 1$

The coefficients (6, –7 and 1) add up to 0. That means $f(1) = 0$. (And that applies to any polynomial at all... always.)

So by the factor theorem, if $f(1) = 0$, $(x - 1)$ is a factor. Easy.

Then just factorise it like any quadratic to get this:

$$f(x) = 6x^2 - 7x + 1 = (6x - 1)(x - 1)$$

The Remainder Theorem is just a factor life...

The Remainder Theorem and Factor Theorem are easy. To be honest, the Remainder Theorem's not a whole heap of use except for checking that you've done your algebraic division right. The Factor Theorem is worth practising a fair bit, though, since it can make factorising quadratics and cubics a whole lot easier and quicker.

Factorising Cubics

Factorising a quadratic function is okay — but you might also be asked to factorise a cubic (something with x^3 in it). And that takes a bit more time — there are more steps, so there are more chances to make mistakes.

Factorising a cubic given One Factor

$$f(x) = 2x^3 + x^2 - 8x - 4$$

Factorising a cubic means exactly what it meant with a quadratic — putting brackets in.
When they ask you to factorise a cubic function, they'll usually tell you one of the factors.

EXAMPLE: Given that $(x + 2)$ is a factor of $f(x) = 2x^3 + x^2 - 8x - 4$, express $f(x)$ as the product of three linear factors.

① The first step is to find a quadratic factor. So write down the factor you know, along with another set of brackets.

$$(x+2)(\qquad) = 2x^3 + x^2 - 8x - 4$$

Put the x^2 bit in this new set of brackets.
These have to multiply together to give you this.

$$(x+2)(2x^2 \qquad) = 2x^3 + x^2 - 8x - 4$$

Factorising Cubics

1) **Find a factor, (if you need to) by finding $f(0)$, $f(\pm1)$, $f(\pm2)$,... until you find $f(k) = 0$. Then $(x - k)$ is a factor.**

2) **Put in the x^2 term.**

3) **Put in the constant.**

4) **Put in the x term by comparing the number of x's on both sides.**

5) **Check there are the same number of x^2's on both sides.**

6) **Factorise the quadratic you've found — if that's possible.**

② Find the number for the second set of brackets. These have to multiply together to give you this.

$$(x+2)(2x^2 \qquad -2) = 2x^3 + x^2 - 8x - 4$$

③ These multiplied give you $-2x$, but there's $-8x$ in $f(x)$ — so you need an 'extra' $-6x$. And that's what this $-3x$ is for.

$$(x+2)(2x^2 - 3x - 2) = 2x^3 + x^2 - 8x - 4$$

You only need $-3x$ because it's going to be multiplied by 2, which makes $-6x$.

If you wanted to solve a cubic equation, you'd do it exactly the same way — put it in the form $ax^3 + bx^2 + cx + d = 0$ and factorise.

④ Before you go any further, check that there are the same number of x^2's on both sides.

$4x^2$ from here...

$$(x+2)(2x^2 - 3x - 2) = 2x^3 + x^2 - 8x - 4$$

...and $-3x^2$ from here...   ...add together to give this x^2.

If this is okay, factorise the quadratic into two linear factors.

$$(2x^2 - 3x - 2) = (2x+1)(x-2)$$

And so... $2x^3 + x^2 - 8x - 4 = (x+2)(2x+1)(x-2)$

Factorising a cubic given No Factors

If they don't give you the first factor, you have to find it yourself. But it's okay — they'll give you an easy one. The best way to find a factor is to guess — use trial and error.

Find f(1) If the answer is zero, you know $(x - 1)$ is a factor.
If the answer isn't zero, find $f(-1)$. If that's zero, then $(x + 1)$ is a factor.

If that doesn't work, keep trying small numbers (find $f(2)$, $f(-2)$, $f(3)$, $f(-3)$ and so on) until you find a number that gives you zero when you put it in the cubic. Call that number k.

$(x - k)$ is a factor of the cubic (from the Factor Theorem).

I love the smell of fresh factorised cubics in the morning...

Factorising cubics is exactly the same as learning to unicycle... It's impossible at first. But when you finally manage it, it's really easy from then onwards and you'll never forget it. Probably. To tell the truth, I can't unicycle at all. So don't believe a word I say.

Section One Revision Questions

And that was Section One ladies and gentlemen — short and sweet. (Well... I say sweet...)
Make sure you can answer all these questions before you move on to Section Two, though.
If you can't do the basic stuff you'll be up s... ahem... you'll struggle come exam time.

1) Work out the following:
   a) $(x^3 + 4x^2 - x + 3) \div (x - 1)$
   b) $(-2x^3 - 2x^2 + 4x - 6) \div (x + 3)$

2) Write the following functions f(x) in the form $f(x) = (x + 2)g(x) + \text{remainder}$ (where g(x) is a quadratic):
   a) $f(x) = 3x^3 - 4x^2 - 5x - 6$,
   b) $f(x) = x^3 + 2x^2 - 3x + 4$

3) Find the remainder when the following are divided by: (i) $(x + 1)$,   (ii) $(x - 1)$
   a) $f(x) = 6x^3 - x^2 - 3x - 12$,
   b) $f(x) = x^4 + 2x^3 - x^2 + 3x + 4$

4) Show that $(x + 2)$ is a factor of $x^3 + 5x^2 + 2x - 8$.

5) a) Show that $(3x - 1)$ is a factor of $3x^3 + 23x^2 + 37x - 15$.
   b) Factorise $x^3 - x^2 - 4x + 4$ into three factors.

6) Find the values of *c* and *d* so that $2x^4 + 3x^3 + 5x^2 + cx + d$ is exactly divisible by $(x - 2)(x + 3)$.

Arc Length and Sector Area

Arc lengths and sector areas are easier than you'd think — once you've learnt two simple(ish) formulas.

Always work in **Radians** for **Arc Length** and **Sector Area Questions**

Remember — for arc length and sector area questions you've got to measure all the angles in radians.
The main thing is that you know how radians relate to degrees.
In short, 180 degrees = π radians. The table below shows you how to convert between the two units:

Converting angles	
<u>Radians to degrees:</u>	<u>Degrees to radians:</u>
Divide by π, multiply by 180.	Divide by 180, multiply by π.

Here's a table of some of the common angles you're going to need — in degrees and radians:

Degrees	0	30	45	60	90	120	180	270	360
Radians	0	$\dfrac{\pi}{6}$	$\dfrac{\pi}{4}$	$\dfrac{\pi}{3}$	$\dfrac{\pi}{2}$	$\dfrac{2\pi}{3}$	π	$\dfrac{3\pi}{2}$	2π

If you have part of a circle (like a section of pie chart), you can work out the length of the curved side, or the area of the 'slice of pie' — as long as you know the angle at the centre (θ) and the length of the radius (r). Read on...

You can find the **Length** of an **Arc** using a nice easy formula...

For a circle with a radius of r, where the angle θ is measured in radians, the arc length of the sector S is given by:

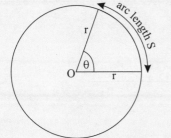

$$S = r\theta$$

If you put θ = 2π in this formula (and so make the sector equal to the whole circle), you get that the distance all the way round the outside of the circle is S = 2πr.

This is just the normal circumference formula.

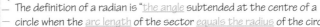
The definition of a radian is "the angle subtended at the centre of a circle when the arc length of the sector equals the radius of the circle".

...and the area of a **Sector** using a similar formula

For a circle with a radius of r, where the angle θ is measured in radians, you can work out A, the area of the sector, using:

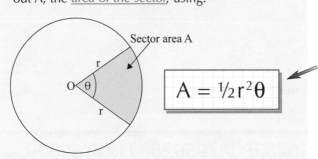
Sector area A

$$A = \tfrac{1}{2}r^2\theta$$

Again, if you put θ = 2π in the formula, you find that the area of the whole circle is A = ½r² × 2π = πr².

This is just the normal 'area of a circle' formula.

Arc Length and Sector Area

Questions on <u>trigonometry</u> quite often use the same angles — so it makes life easier if you know the sin, cos and tan of these commonly used angles. Or to put it another way, examiners expect you to know them — so learn them.

Draw Triangles to remember sin, cos and tan of the Important Angles

You should know the values of <u>sin</u>, <u>cos</u> and <u>tan</u> at 30°, 60° and 45°. But to help you remember, you can draw these two groovy triangles. It may seem a complicated way to learn a few numbers, but it does make it easier. Honest.

The idea is you draw the triangles below, putting in their angles and side lengths. Then you can use them to work out special trig values like <u>sin 45°</u> or <u>cos 60°</u> more accurately than any calculator (which only gives a few decimal places).

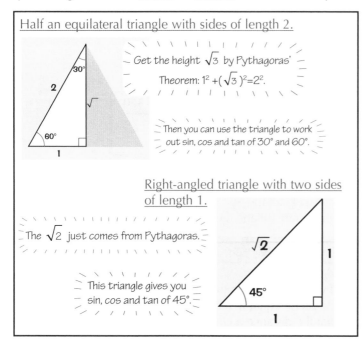

Half an equilateral triangle with sides of length 2.

Get the height $\sqrt{3}$ by Pythagoras' Theorem: $1^2 + (\sqrt{3})^2 = 2^2$.

Then you can use the triangle to work out sin, cos and tan of 30° and 60°.

Right-angled triangle with two sides of length 1.

The $\sqrt{2}$ just comes from Pythagoras.

This triangle gives you sin, cos and tan of 45°.

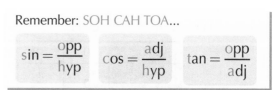

Remember: SOH CAH TOA...

$$\sin = \frac{\text{opp}}{\text{hyp}} \qquad \cos = \frac{\text{adj}}{\text{hyp}} \qquad \tan = \frac{\text{opp}}{\text{adj}}$$

Trig Values from Triangles

$\sin 30° = \dfrac{1}{2}$	$\sin 60° = \dfrac{\sqrt{3}}{2}$	$\sin 45° = \dfrac{1}{\sqrt{2}}$
$\cos 30° = \dfrac{\sqrt{3}}{2}$	$\cos 60° = \dfrac{1}{2}$	$\cos 45° = \dfrac{1}{\sqrt{2}}$
$\tan 30° = \dfrac{1}{\sqrt{3}}$	$\tan 60° = \sqrt{3}$	$\tan 45° = 1$

Example: Find the exact length L and area A in the diagram.

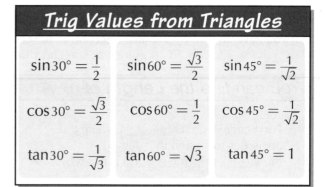

Right, first things first... it's an arc length and sector area, so you need the angle in radians.

$$45° = \frac{45 \times \pi}{180} = \frac{\pi}{4} \text{ radians}$$

Or you could just quote this if you've learnt the stuff above.

Now bung everything in your formulas:

$$L = r\theta = 20 \times \frac{\pi}{4} = 5\pi \text{ cm}$$

$$A = \frac{1}{2}r^2\theta = \frac{1}{2} \times 20^2 \times \frac{\pi}{4} = 50\pi \text{ cm}^2$$

Example: Find the area of the shaded part of the symbol.

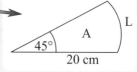

You need the area of the 'leaves' and so use the formula $\frac{1}{2}r^2\theta$.

Each leaf has area $\frac{1}{2} \times 10^2 \times \frac{\pi}{4} = 25\frac{\pi}{2} \text{ cm}^2$

So the area of the whole symbol $= 4 \times 25\frac{\pi}{2} = 50\pi \text{ cm}^2$

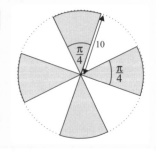

π = 3.14159265358979323846264338327950288419716 9399...(Make sure you know it)

It's worth repeating, just to make sure — those formulas for arc length and sector area only work if the angle is in <u>radians</u>.

The Trig Formulas You Need to Know

There are some more trig formulas you need to know for the exam.
So here they are — learn them or you're seriously stuffed. Worse than an aubergine.

The **Sine Rule** and **Cosine Rule** work for **Any** triangle

Remember these three formulas work for <u>ANY</u> triangle, not just right-angled ones.

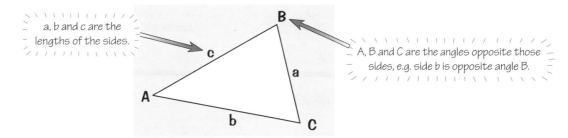

a, b and c are the lengths of the sides.

A, B and C are the angles opposite those sides, e.g. side b is opposite angle B.

THE SINE RULE
$\dfrac{a}{\sin A} = \dfrac{b}{\sin B} = \dfrac{c}{\sin C}$

THE COSINE RULE
$a^2 = b^2 + c^2 - 2bc\cos A$

AREA OF ANY TRIANGLE
$Area = \frac{1}{2}ab\sin C$

Sine Rule or *Cosine Rule* — which one is it...

To decide which of these two rules you need to use, look at how much you <u>already</u> know about the triangle.

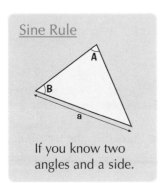

Sine Rule

If you know two angles and a side.

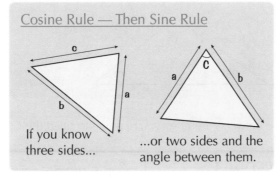

Cosine Rule — Then Sine Rule

If you know three sides...

...or two sides and the angle between them.

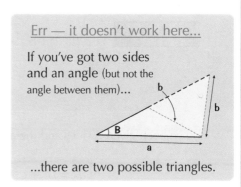

Err — it doesn't work here...

If you've got two sides and an angle (but not the angle between them)...

...there are two possible triangles.

The **Best** has been saved till last...

These two identities are really important. You'll need them <u>loads</u>.

$\tan x \equiv \dfrac{\sin x}{\cos x}$

$$\sin^2 x + \cos^2 x \equiv 1$$

$$\Rightarrow \sin^2 x \equiv 1 - \cos^2 x$$
$$\cos^2 x \equiv 1 - \sin^2 x$$

Work out these two using $\sin^2 + \cos^2 \equiv 1$.

These two come up in exam questions <u>all the time</u>. Learn them.
Learnthemlearnthemlearnthemlearnthemlearnthemlear... okay, I'll stop now.

Tri angles — go on... you might like them.

Formulas and trigonometry go together even better than Richard and Judy. I can count 7 on this page. That's not many, so please, just make sure you know them! If you haven't learned them I will cry for you. I will sob.

Using the Sine and Cosine Rules

This page is about "solving" triangles, which just means finding all their sides and angles when you already know a few.

EXAMPLE: Solve $\triangle$ ABC, in which A=40°, a=27 m, B=73°. Then find the area.

Draw a quick sketch first — don't worry if it's not deadly accurate, though.
You're given 2 angles and a side, so you need the Sine Rule.

> Make sure you put side
> a opposite angle A.

First of all, get the other angle: $\angle C = (180 - 40 - 73)° = 67°$

Then find the other sides, one at a time (giving the answer to 1 d.p.):

$$\frac{a}{\sin A} = \frac{b}{\sin B} \Rightarrow \frac{27}{\sin 40°} = \frac{b}{\sin 73°}$$
$$\Rightarrow b = \frac{\sin 73°}{\sin 40°} \times 27 = \underline{40.2\,\text{m}}$$

$$\frac{c}{\sin C} = \frac{a}{\sin A} \Rightarrow \frac{c}{\sin 67°} = \frac{27}{\sin 40°}$$
$$\Rightarrow c = \frac{\sin 67°}{\sin 40°} \times 27 = \underline{38.7\,\text{m}}$$

Now just use the formula to find its area.

$$\text{Area of } \triangle \text{ ABC} = \tfrac{1}{2}ab\sin C$$
$$= \tfrac{1}{2} \times 27 \times 40.169 \times \sin 67°$$
$$= \underline{499.2\,\text{m}^2}$$

> Use a more accurate value for b here,
> rather than the rounded value 40.2.

EXAMPLE: Find X, Y and z.

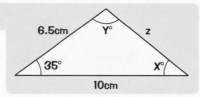

You've been given 2 sides and the angle between them, so you're going to need the Cosine Rule, then the Sine Rule.

$$\boxed{a^2 = b^2 + c^2 - 2bc\cos A}$$

$$\boxed{\frac{a}{\sin A} = \frac{b}{\sin B} = \frac{c}{\sin C}}$$

$$z^2 = (6.5)^2 + 10^2 - 2(6.5)(10)\cos 35°$$
$$\Rightarrow z^2 = 142.25 - 130\cos 35°$$
$$\Rightarrow z^2 = 35.7602$$
$$\Rightarrow z = \underline{5.98\,\text{cm}} \text{ (to 2 d.p.)}$$

> In this case, angle A is 35°,
> and side a is actually z.

You've got all the sides. Now use the Sine Rule to find the other two angles (to 1 d.p.).

> The Sine Rule just says:
> Dividing "length of a side" by "the sine
> of the opposite angle" gives the same
> answer, whichever pair you choose.

$$\frac{6.5}{\sin X} = \frac{5.9800}{\sin 35°}$$
$$\Rightarrow \sin X = 0.6235$$
$$\Rightarrow X = \sin^{-1} 0.6235$$
$$\Rightarrow \underline{X = 38.6°}$$

$$\frac{10}{\sin Y} = \frac{5.9800}{\sin 35°}$$
$$\Rightarrow \sin Y = 0.9592$$
$$\Rightarrow Y = \sin^{-1} 0.9592$$
$$\Rightarrow Y = 73.6° \text{ or } \underline{106.4°}$$

> This is the answer you need.
> Be careful: your calculator
> only gives you values for $\sin^{-1}$
> between −90° and 90°.

Check your answers by adding up all the angles in the triangle. If they don't add up to 180°, you've gone wrong somewhere.

Graphs of Trig Functions

Before you leave this page, you should be able to close your eyes and picture these three graphs in your head, properly labelled and everything. If you can't, you need to learn them more. I'm not kidding.

sin x and cos x are always in the range –1 to 1

sin x and cos x are similar — they just bob up and down between –1 and 1.

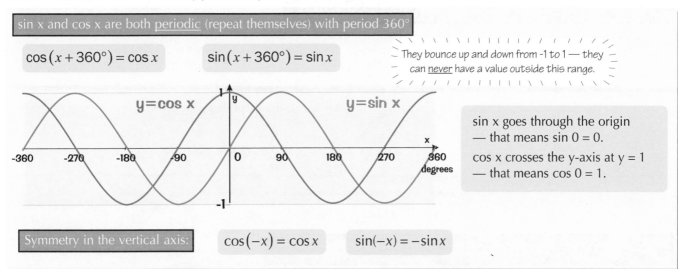

sin x and cos x are both <u>periodic</u> (repeat themselves) with period 360°

$$\cos(x + 360°) = \cos x \qquad \sin(x + 360°) = \sin x$$

They bounce up and down from -1 to 1 — they can <u>never</u> have a value outside this range.

y=cos x   y=sin x

sin x goes through the origin — that means sin 0 = 0.

cos x crosses the y-axis at y = 1 — that means cos 0 = 1.

Symmetry in the vertical axis: $\cos(-x) = \cos x$ $\sin(-x) = -\sin x$

tan x can be Any Value at all

tan x is different from sin x or cos x.
It doesn't go gently up and down between –1 and 1 — it goes between $-\infty$ and $+\infty$.

TAN X IS ALSO <u>PERIODIC</u> — BUT WITH PERIOD 180°

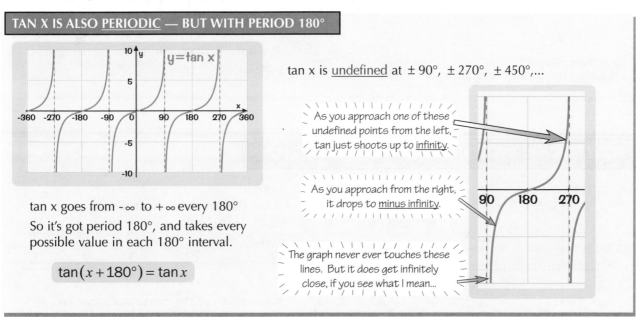

y=tan x

tan x is <u>undefined</u> at $\pm 90°$, $\pm 270°$, $\pm 450°$,...

As you approach one of these undefined points from the left, tan just shoots up to <u>infinity</u>.

As you approach from the right, it drops to <u>minus infinity</u>.

tan x goes from $-\infty$ to $+\infty$ every 180°

So it's got period 180°, and takes every possible value in each 180° interval.

$$\tan(x + 180°) = \tan x$$

The graph never ever touches these lines. But it does get infinitely close, if you see what I mean...

The easiest way to sketch any of these graphs is to plot the important points which happen every 90° (i.e. –180°, –90°, 0°, 90°, 180°, 270°, 360°...) and then just join the dots up.

Sin and cos can make your life worthwhile — give them a chance...

It's really really really really really important that you can draw the trig graphs on this page, and get all the labels right. Make sure you know what value sin, cos and tan have at the interesting points — i.e. 0°, 90°, 180°, 270°, 360°. It's easy to remember what the graphs look like, but you've got to know exactly <u>where</u> they're max, min, zero, etc.

Transformed Trig Graphs

Transformed trigonometric graphs look much the same as the bog standard ones, just a little different.
There are three main types, vertical or horizontal stretches or translation along an axis.

There are 3 basic types of Transformed Trig Graph...

$y = n\sin x$ — a Vertical Stretch or Squash

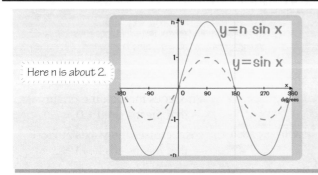

Here n is about 2.

If n > 1, the graph of y = sin x is <u>stretched vertically</u> by a factor of n.

If 0 < n < 1, the graph is <u>squashed</u>.

And if n < 0, the graph is also <u>reflected</u> in the <u>x-axis</u>.

$y = \sin nx$ — a Horizontal Squash or Stretch

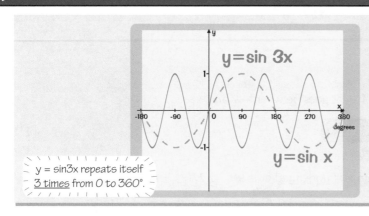

y = sin3x repeats itself <u>3 times</u> from 0 to 360°.

If n > 1, the graph of y = sin x is <u>squashed horizontally</u> by a factor of n.

If 0 < n < 1, the graph is <u>stretched</u>.

And if n < 0, the graph is also <u>reflected</u> in the <u>y-axis</u>.

$y = \sin(x + c)$ — a Translation along the x-axis

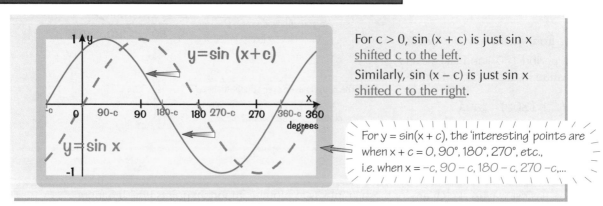

For c > 0, sin (x + c) is just sin x <u>shifted c to the left</u>.

Similarly, sin (x − c) is just sin x <u>shifted c to the right</u>.

For y = sin(x + c), the 'interesting' points are when x + c = 0, 90°, 180°, 270°, etc., i.e. when x = −c, 90 − c, 180 − c, 270 − c,...

Curling up on the sofa with 2cos x — that's my idea of cosiness ☺

One thing you've really got to be careful about is making sure you move or stretch the graphs in the right direction.
In that last example, the graph would have moved to the right if "c" was negative. And it gets confusing with the horizontal
and vertical stretching and squashing — in the first two examples above, n > 1 means a <u>vertical stretch</u> for one but a
<u>horizontal squash</u> for the other — so make sure you know which is which.

Solving Trig Equations in a Given Interval

I used to really hate trig stuff like this. But once I'd got the hang of it, I just couldn't get enough. I stopped going out, lost interest in the opposite sex — the CAST method became my life. Learn it, but be careful. It's addictive.

There are **Two Ways** to find Solutions in an **Interval**...

EXAMPLE: Solve $\cos x = \frac{1}{2}$ for $-360° \le x \le 720°$.

Like I said — there are two ways to solve this kind of question. Just use the one you prefer...

You can draw a graph...

Your calculator gives you a solution of 60° (but see page 6 if you didn't know this anyway). Then you have to work out what the others will be. The other solutions are 60° either side of the graph's peaks.

1) Draw the graph of $y = \cos x$ for the range you're interested in...

2) Get the first solution from your calculator and mark this on the graph,

3) Use the symmetry of the graph to work out what the other solutions are:

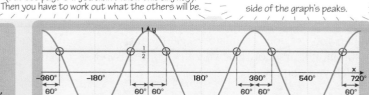

So the solutions are: $-300°$, $-60°$, $60°$, $300°$, $420°$ and $660°$.

...or you can use the **CAST** diagram

CAST stands for COS, ALL, SIN, TAN — and the CAST diagram shows you where these functions are positive:

Between 90° and 180°, only SIN is positive.

Between 0 and 90°, ALL of sin, cos and tan are positive.

Between 180° and 270°, only TAN is positive.

Between 270° and 360°, only COS is positive.

This is positive — so you're only interested in where cos is positive.

First, to find all the values of x between 0° and 360° where $\cos x = \frac{1}{2}$ — you do this:

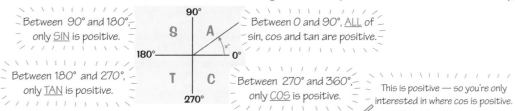

Put the first solution onto the CAST diagram.	Find the other angles between 0° and 360° that might be solutions.	Ditch the ones that are the wrong sign.

The angle from your calculator goes anticlockwise from the x-axis (unless it's negative — then it would go clockwise into the 4th quadrant).

The other solutions come from making the same angle from the horizontal axis into the other 3 quadrants.

$\cos x = \frac{1}{2}$, which is positive. The CAST diagram tells you cos is positive in the 4th quadrant — but not the 2nd or 3rd — so ditch those two angles.

So you've got solutions 60° and 300° in the range 0° to 360°. But you need all the solutions in the range $-360°$ to 720°. Get these by repeatedly adding or subtracting 360° onto each until you go out of range:

$x = 60° \Rightarrow$ (adding 360°) $x = 420°$, 780° (too big)

and (subtracting 360°) $x = -300°$, $-660°$ (too small)

$x = 300° \Rightarrow$ (adding 360°) $x = 660°$, 1020° (too big)

and (subtracting 360°) $x = -60$, $-420°$ (too small)

So the solutions are: $x = -300°$, $-60°$, $60°$, $300°$, $420°$ and $660°$.

And I feel that love is dead, I'm loving angles instead...

Suppose the first solution you get is negative, let's say $-d°$, then you'd measure it clockwise on the CAST diagram. So it'd be d° in the 4th quadrant. Then you'd work out the other 3 possible solutions in exactly the same way, rejecting the ones which weren't the right sign. Got that? No? Got that? No? Got that? Yes? Good!

SECTION TWO — TRIGONOMETRY

Solving Trig Equations in a Given Interval

Sometimes it's a bit more complicated. But only a bit.

Sometimes you end up with *sin kx = number*...

For these, it's definitely easier to draw the <u>graph</u> rather than use the CAST method — that's one reason why being able to sketch these trig graphs properly is so important.

EXAMPLE: Solve: $\sin 3x = -\dfrac{1}{\sqrt{2}}$ for $0° \le x \le 360°$.

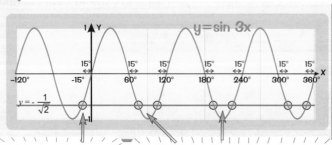

1) You've got 3x instead of x — so when you draw the graph, make it three times as <u>squashed</u> (the period will be 120° instead of 360°).

2) When you use your calculator to get the first solution, it'll probably give you a <u>negative</u> answer (which you don't want).

$$\sin 3x = -\frac{1}{\sqrt{2}}$$
$$\Rightarrow 3x = -45°$$
$$\Rightarrow x = -15°$$

You don't want this solution — so use your graph to work out one that you do want.

This is the solution your calculator gives you...

...but these are the solutions you actually want — they're all 15° from a point where the graph crosses the x-axis.

3) Using the <u>symmetry</u> of the graph, you can see that the solutions you want are:

   x = 75°, 105°, 195°, 225°, 315° and 345°.

   It really is mega-important that you check these answers — it's dead easy to make a silly mistake.

4) <u>Check</u> your answers by putting these values back into your calculator.

...or *sin (x + k)= number*

All the steps in this example are just the same as in the one above.

EXAMPLE: Solve $\sin(x + 60°) = \dfrac{3}{4}$ for $-360° \le x \le 360°$, giving your answers to 2 decimal places.

1) You've got sin (x + 60°) instead of sin x — so when you draw the graph, you have to move it 60° to the <u>left</u>.

2) Use your calculator to get that first solution...

$$\sin(x+60°) = \frac{3}{4}$$
$$\Rightarrow x + 60° = 48.59°$$
$$\Rightarrow x = -11.41°$$

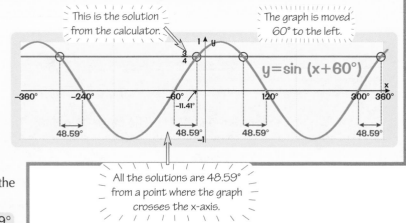

This is the solution from the calculator.

The graph is moved 60° to the left.

All the solutions are 48.59° from a point where the graph crosses the x-axis.

3) And again, use the graph's <u>symmetry</u> to get the other three. The solutions are:

   $x = -11.41°, -288.59°, 71.41°$ and $348.59°$

4) <u>Check</u> your answers by putting these values back into your calculator.

Live a life of sin (and cos and tan)...

Yep, the examples on this page are pretty fiddly. The most important bit is actually getting the sketch right. If you don't, you're in big trouble. Then you've just got to carefully use the sketch to work out the other solutions. It's tricky, but you'll feel better about yourself when you've got it mastered. Ah you will, you will, you will ...

Solving Trig Equations in a Given Interval

Now for something really exciting — trig identities. Mmm, well, maybe exciting was the wrong word.
But they can be dead useful, so here goes...

For equations with *tan x* in, it often helps to use this...

$$\tan x \equiv \frac{\sin x}{\cos x}$$

This is a handy thing to know — and one the examiners love testing. Basically, if you've got a trig equation with a tan in it, together with a sin or a cos — chances are you'll be better off if you rewrite the tan using this formula.

EXAMPLE: Solve: $3\sin x - \tan x = 0$, for $0 \leq x \leq 2\pi$.

It's got sin and tan in it — so writing tan x as $\dfrac{\sin x}{\cos x}$ is probably a good move:

$$3\sin x - \tan x = 0$$

$$\Rightarrow 3\sin x - \frac{\sin x}{\cos x} = 0$$

Get rid of the cos x on the bottom by multiplying the whole equation by cos x.

$$\Rightarrow 3\sin x \cos x - \sin x = 0$$

Now — there's a common factor of sin x. Take that outside a bracket.

$$\Rightarrow \sin x(3\cos x - 1) = 0$$

And now you're almost there. You've got two things multiplying together to make zero. That means either one or both of them is equal to zero themselves.

$$\Rightarrow \sin x = 0 \quad \text{or} \quad 3\cos x - 1 = 0$$

Don't forget to put your calculator in the radian mode for questions involving radians.

$\boxed{\sin x = 0}$

The first solution is...   **sin 0 = 0**

Now find the other points where sin x is zero in the interval $0 \leq x \leq 2\pi$.
(Remember the sin graph is zero every π radians.)

$$\Rightarrow x = 0, \pi, 2\pi \text{ radians}$$

$\boxed{3\cos x - 1 = 0}$

CAST gives any solutions in the interval $0 \leq x \leq 2\pi$.

Rearrange... $\cos x = \frac{1}{3}$

So the first solution is...

$$\cos^{-1}\tfrac{1}{3} = 1.231$$

CAST (or the graph of cos x) gives another solution in the 4th quadrant...

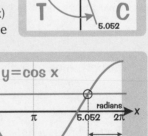

So altogether you've got <u>five</u> possible solutions:

$$\Rightarrow x = 0, \pi, 2\pi, 1.231, 5.052 \text{ radians}$$

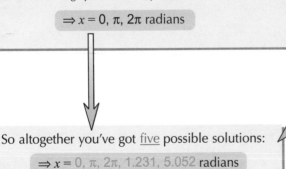

And the two solutions from this part are:

$$\Rightarrow x = 1.231, 5.052 \text{ radians}$$

Trigonometry is the root of all evil...

What a page — you don't have fun like that every day, do you? No, trig equations are where it's at. This is a really useful trick, though — and can turn a nightmare of an equation into a bit of a pussy-cat. Rewriting stuff using different formulas is always worth trying if it feels like you're getting stuck — even if you're not sure why when you're doing it. You might have a flash of inspiration when you see the new version.

Solving Trig Equations in a Given Interval

Another trig identity — and it's a good 'un — examiners love it. And it's not difficult either.

And if you have a sin² x or a cos² x, think of this straight away...

$$\sin^2 x + \cos^2 x \equiv 1 \implies \begin{array}{l} \sin^2 x \equiv 1 - \cos^2 x \\ \cos^2 x \equiv 1 - \sin^2 x \end{array}$$

Use this identity to get rid of a sin² or a cos² that's making things awkward...

EXAMPLE: Solve: $2\sin^2 x + 5\cos x = 4$, for $0° \leq x \leq 360°$.

You can't do much while the equation's got both sin's and cos's in it. So replace the sin²x bit with $1 - \cos^2 x$.

$$2(1 - \cos^2 x) + 5\cos x = 4$$

Multiply out the bracket and rearrange it so that you've got zero on one side — and you get a quadratic in cos x:

Now the only trig function is cos.

$$\Rightarrow 2 - 2\cos^2 x + 5\cos x = 4$$
$$\Rightarrow 2\cos^2 x - 5\cos x + 2 = 0$$

If you replaced cos x with y, this would be $2y^2 - 5y + 2 = 0$.

This is a quadratic in cos x. It's easier to factorise this if you make the substitution $y = \cos x$.

$$2y^2 - 5y + 2 = 0$$
$$\Rightarrow (2y - 1)(y - 2) = 0$$
$$\Rightarrow (2\cos x - 1)(\cos x - 2) = 0$$

$2y^2 - 5y + 2 = (2y \quad ?)(y \quad ?)$
$= (2y - 1)(y - 2)$

Now one of the brackets must be 0. So you get 2 equations as usual:

$$(2\cos x - 1) = 0 \quad or \quad (\cos x - 2) = 0$$

This is a bit weird. cos x is always between −1 and 1. So you don't get any solutions from this bracket.

$$\cos x = \tfrac{1}{2} \Rightarrow x = 60° \quad or \quad x = 300° \quad and \quad \cos x = 2$$

This is impossible — so you get nothing from this bracket.

So at the end of all that, the only solutions you get are x = 60° and x = 300°. How boring.

Use the Trig Identities to prove something is the Same as something else

Another use for these trig identities is proving that two things are the same.

EXAMPLE: Show that $\dfrac{\cos^2 \theta}{1 + \sin \theta} \equiv 1 - \sin \theta$

The identity sign ≡ means that this is true for all θ, rather than just certain values.

Prove things like this by playing about with one side of the equation until you get the other side.

Left-hand side: $\dfrac{\cos^2 \theta}{1 + \sin \theta}$

The only thing I can think of doing here is replacing cos² θ with $1 - \sin^2 \theta$. (Which is good because it works.)

$$\equiv \frac{1 - \sin^2 \theta}{1 + \sin \theta}$$

The next trick is the hardest to spot. Look at the top — does that remind you of anything?

The top line is a difference of two squares:

$$\equiv \frac{(1 + \sin \theta)(1 - \sin \theta)}{1 + \sin \theta}$$

$1 - a^2 = (1 + a)(1 - a)$
$\Rightarrow 1 - \sin^2 \theta = (1 + \sin \theta)(1 - \sin \theta)$

$$\equiv 1 - \sin \theta, \text{ the right-hand side.}$$

Trig identities — the path to a brighter future...

That was a pretty miserable section. But it's over. These trig identities aren't exactly a barrel of laughs, but they are a definite source of marks — you can bet your last penny they'll be in the exam. That substitution trick to get rid of a sin² or a cos² and end up with a quadratic in sin x or cos x is a real examiners' favourite. Those identities can be a bit daunting, but it's always worth having a few tricks in the back of your mind — always look for things that factorise, or fractions that can be cancelled down, or ways to use those trig identities. Ah, it's all good clean fun.

Section Two Revision Questions

Welcome to <u>Who wants to be a Mathematician</u> — the page that gives you the chance to win a million marks in your exam by answering questions on a topic of your choice. You have chosen Section Two — Trigonometry...

For £100:   Draw a triangle $\triangle XYZ$ with sides of length x, y and z. Write down the Sine and Cosine Rules for this triangle. Write down an expression for its area.

For £200:   Write down the exact values of cos 30°, sin 30°, tan 30°, cos 45°, sin 45°, tan 45°, cos 60°, sin 60°, tan 60°. (You'll probably want to draw a couple of triangles to help you.)

For £300:   What is tan x in terms of cos x and sin x? What is $\cos^2 x$ in terms of $\sin^2 x$?

For £500:   Solve a) $\triangle ABC$ in which A = 30°, C = 25°, b = 6m and find its area.
                   b) $\triangle PQR$ in which p = 3 km, q = 23 km, R = 10°.   (answers to 2 d.p.)

For £1000:   My pet triangle Freda has sides of length 10, 20, 25. Find her angles (to 1 d.p.) and sketch her.

Well done — you now have a guaranteed win of £1000.

For £2000:   Find the 2 possible triangles $\triangle ABC$ which satisfy b = 5, a = 3, A = 35°. (This is tricky: Sketch it first, and see if you can work out how to make 2 different triangles satisfying the data given.)

For £4000:   Sketch the graphs for sin x, cos x and tan x.
                   Make sure you label all the max/min/zero/undefined points.

For £8000:   Sketch the following graphs:

            a) y = ½ cos 2x   (for 0° ≤ x ≤ 360°)   b) y = 2 sin (x+30°)   (for 0° ≤ x ≤ 360°)

            c) y = tan 3x   (for 0° ≤ x ≤ 180°)

For £16 000:   Solve each of these equations for 0° ≤ θ ≤ 360°:

            a) $\sin\theta = -\frac{\sqrt{3}}{2}$ b) $\tan\theta = -1$ c) $\cos\theta = -\frac{1}{\sqrt{2}}$ *I such*

For £32 000:   Solve each of these equations for -180° ≤ θ ≤ 180° (giving your answer to 1 d.p.):

            a) $\cos 4\theta = -\frac{2}{3}$ b) $\sin(\theta + 35) = 0.3$ c) $\tan(\frac{1}{2}\theta) = 500$

Congratulations! You will now be taking home a cheque for at least £32000!

For £64 000:   Find all the solutions to $6\sin^2 x = \cos x + 5$ in the range 0° ≤ x ≤ 400° (answers to 1 d.p.).

For £125 000:   Solve $3\tan x + 2\cos x = 0$ for -90° ≤ x ≤ 90°

For £250 000:   Simplify: $(\sin y + \cos y)^2 + (\cos y - \sin y)^2$

For £500 000:   Show that $\dfrac{\sin^4 x + \sin^2 x \cos^2 x}{\cos^2 x - 1} \equiv -1$

Here comes the big one. Are you ready?

For £1 million: Which of the following identities is correct?

           A $\sin^2 x + \cos^2 x \equiv \tan^2 x$ B $\sin^2 x - \cos^2 x \equiv 1$

           C $\sin^2 ☺ + \cos^2 ☠ \equiv ✌$ D $\sin^2 x + \cos^2 x \equiv 1$

Are you sure? Is that your final answer? Perhaps you'd like to phone a teacher.

Well I can tell you, if you <u>had</u> said C........

.... you would have just <u>lost</u> £468,000...

Logs

Don't be put off by your parents or grandparents telling you that logs are hard. Logarithm is just a fancy word for power, and once you know how to use them you can solve all sorts of equations.

You need to be able to **Switch** between **Different Notations**

$$\log_a b = c \text{ means the same as } a^c = b$$

$$\text{That means that } \log_a a = 1 \text{ and } \log_a 1 = 0$$

The little number 'a' after 'log' is called the base.
Logs can be to any base, but base 10 is the most common.
The button marked 'log' on your calculator uses base 10.

Example: Index notation: $10^2 = 100$ log notation: $\log_{10} 100 = 2$

The base goes here but it's usually left out if it's 10.

So the logarithm of 100 to the base 10 is 2, because 10 raised to the power of 2 is 100.

Examples:

Write down the values of the following:

a) $\log_2 8$ b) $\log_9 3$ c) $\log_5 5$

a) 8 is 2 raised to the power of 3
  so $2^3 = 8$ and $\log_2 8 = 3$

b) 3 is the square root of 9, or $9^{1/2} = 3$
  so $\log_9 3 = 1/2$

c) anything to the power of 1 is itself
  so $\log_5 5 = 1$

Write the following using log notation:

a) $5^3 = 125$ b) $3^0 = 1$

You just need to make sure you get things in the right place.

a) 3 is the power or logarithm that 5
  (the base) is raised to to get 125
  so $\log_5 125 = 3$

b) you'll need to remember this one:
  $\log_3 1 = 0$

The **Laws of Logarithms** are **Unbelievably Useful**

Whenever you have to deal with logs (or for that matter exponentials), you'll end up using the laws below. That means it's not a bad idea to learn them off by heart right now.

Laws of Logarithms

$$\log_a x + \log_a y = \log_a (xy)$$

$$\log_a x - \log_a y = \log_a \left(\frac{x}{y}\right)$$

$$\log_a x^k = k \log_a x$$

Use the **Laws** to **Manipulate Logs**

Example: Write each expression in the form $\log_a n$, where n is a number.

a) $\log_a 5 + \log_a 4$ b) $2 \log_a 6 - \log_a 9$

a) $\log_a x + \log_a y = \log_a (xy)$

You just have to multiply the numbers together:

$\log_a 5 + \log_a 4 = \log_a (5 \times 4)$
$= \log_a 20$

b) $\log_a x^k = k \log_a x$

$2 \log_a 6 = \log_a 6^2 = \log_a 36$
$\log_a 36 - \log_a 9 = \log_a (36 \div 9)$
$= \log_a 4$

Exponentials and Logs

Okay, you've done the theory of logs. So now it's a bit of stuff about exponentials (the opposite of logs, kind of)...

Graphs of a^x Never Reach Zero

All the graphs of $y = a^x$ (exponential graphs) where $a > 1$ have the <u>same basic shape</u>.
The graphs for $a = 2$, $a = 3$ and $a = 4$ are shown on the right.

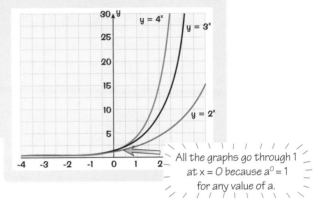

- All the a's are greater than 1 — so <u>y increases as x increases</u>.
- The <u>bigger</u> a is, the <u>quicker</u> the graphs increase.
  The rate at which they increase gets bigger too.
- As x <u>decreases</u>, y <u>decreases</u> at a <u>smaller and smaller rate</u>
  — y will approach zero, but never actually get there.

All the graphs go through 1 at x = 0 because $a^0 = 1$ for any value of a.

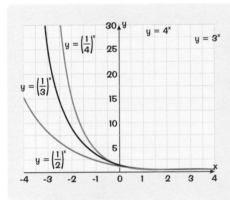

The graphs on the left are for $y = a^x$ where $0 < a < 1$

(they're for $a = \frac{1}{2}, \frac{1}{3}$ and $\frac{1}{4}$).

- All the a's are less than 1 — meaning <u>y decreases as x increases</u>.
- As x <u>increases</u>, y <u>decreases</u> at a <u>smaller and smaller rate</u> —
  again, y will approach zero, but never actually get there.
- In fact, they're reflections in the y-axis of the graphs above.
  If you think about it, this is what you'd expect, since they show
  $y = a^{-x}$ for $a = 2, 3$, and 4 — i.e. they're transformations of the
  form $y = f(-x)$.

Use the Laws of Logarithms to solve *inequalities* like $a^x < b$.

If you've learnt the laws of logarithms (see page 16) you'll find this a piece of cake
— it's just a case of manipulating the exponential expression (a^x) to get the inequality in terms of x.

| Example: | Use logarithms to solve the inequality $8^{2x} < 64$, giving the answers to 4 s.f. |

You could use any base you like — $\log_2$ has been chosen because $\log_2 8 = 3$ and $\log_2 64 = 6$ (makes the calculation easier)

1) Starting with the inequality $8^{2x} < 64$, first log both sides to give:
   $$\log_2 8^{2x} < \log_2 64$$

2) Use the Logarithm Law $\log_a x^k = k\log_a x$ to rewrite the inequality as:
   $$(2x)\log_2 8 < \log_2 64$$

3) Rearrange this to get x on its own:

   $$x < \frac{\log_2 64}{2\log_2 8} \quad \text{which is the same as} \quad x < \frac{6}{2 \times 3}$$

4) So, the answer is $x < 1$

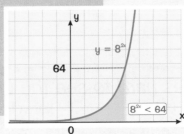

Exponentials and Logs

Now, fingers at the ready, it's time to get your calculator out for a bit of button pressing...

Use the Calculator Log Button Whenever You Can

Example: Use logarithms to solve the following for x, giving the answers to 4 s.f.
a) $10^x = 170$ b) $10^{3x} = 4000$ c) $7^x = 55$ d) $\log_{10}x = 2.6$ e) $\log_2 x = 5$

You've got the magic buttons on your calculator, but you'd better <u>follow the instructions</u> and show that you know how to use the <u>log rules</u> covered earlier.

(a)

$10^x = 170$ — when you get an equation with the 'unknown' in the power, <u>take logs of both sides</u> of the equation (which you do by writing 'log' in front of both sides). Then you can use the <u>laws of logs</u> to fiddle about with the result. In theory, it doesn't matter what <u>base</u> you use, but your calculator has a '$\log_{10}$' button, so base 10 is usually a good idea. But whatever base you use, <u>use the same one for both sides</u>.

So taking logs to base 10 of both sides of the above equation gives:

$\log 10^x = \log 170$
i.e. $x\log 10 = \log 170$
i.e. $x = \log 170 = 2.230$ (to 4 sig. fig)

Since $\log_{10}10 = 1$.

(b)

$10^{3x} = 4000$. Same again — take logs (to base 10) of both sides to get: $3x = \log_{10} 4000 = 3.602$, so $x = 1.201$

(c)

$7^x = 55$. Once again, take logs of both sides, and use the log rules: $x \log_{10}7 = \log_{10}55$, so $x = \dfrac{\log_{10} 55}{\log_{10} 7} = 2.059$

(d)

$\log_{10}x = 2.6$ — to get rid of a log, you 'take exponentials', meaning you do '10 (or the base) to the power of each side'. Think of 'taking logs' and 'taking exponentials' as opposite processes — one cancels the other out: $10^{\log_{10} x} = 10^{2.6}$
i.e. $x = 398.1$

Or you can simply use the formula on p16— whichever you prefer

(e)

$\log_2 x = 5$. Here, the base is 2, so 'taking exponentials' means doing '2 to the power of both sides': $2^{\log_2 x} = 2^5$
i.e. $x = 2^5 = 32$

It's sometimes hard to see the wood for the trees — especially with logs...

Tricky, tricky, tricky... I think of $\log_a b$ as 'the <u>power</u> I have to raise a to if I want to end up with b' — that's all it is. And the log laws make a bit more sense if you think of 'log' as meaning 'power'. For example, you know that $2^a \times 2^b = 2^{a+b}$ — this just says that if you multiply two numbers, you add the powers. Well, the first law of logs is saying the same thing. Any road up, even if you don't really understand why they work, make sure you know the log laws like you know your own navel.

Section Three Revision Questions

Logs* and exponentials are surprisingly useful things. As well as being in your exam they pop up all over the place in real life — savings, radioactive decay, growth of bacteria — all log*arithmic.

And now for something (marginally) different:

1) Write down the values of the following:
   a) $\log_3 27$
   b) $\log_3 (1 \div 27)$
   c) $\log_3 18 - \log_3 2$

2) Simplify the following:
   a) $\log 3 + 2 \log 5$
   b) $\frac{1}{2} \log 36 - \log 3$

3) Simplify $\log_b (\chi^2 - 1) - \log_b (\chi - 1)$

4) Copy and complete the table for the function $y = 4^x$:

x	−3	−2	−1	0	1	2	3
y							

   a) Using suitable scales, plot a graph of $y = 4^x$ for $-3 < x < 3$.
   b) Use the graph to solve the equation $4^x = 20$.

5) Use logarithms to solve the following inequalities:
   a) $27^x > 81$
   b) $16^{(x+1)} < 2$

6) Solve these little jokers:
   a) $10^x = 240$ b) $\log_{10} x = 2.6$
   c) $10^{2x+1} = 1500$ d) $4^{(x-1)} = 200$

7) Find the smallest integer P such that $1.5^P > 1\,000\,000$

* He's a lumberjack and he's okay.
He sleeps all night and he works all day.

Sequences

A sequence is a list of numbers that follow a <u>certain pattern</u>. Sequences can be <u>finite</u> or <u>infinite</u> (infinity — oooh), and they're usually generated in one of two ways. And guess what? You have to know everything about them.

A Sequence can be defined by its nth Term

You may well have covered this stuff at GCSE — if so, you've got <u>no excuses</u> for mucking it up.

With some sequences, you can work out any <u>value</u> (<u>the nth term</u>) from its <u>position</u> in the sequence (<u>n</u>). And often, you can even work out a <u>formula</u> for the nth term.

Example: Find the nth term of the sequence 5, 8, 11, 14, 17, ...

1st	2nd	3rd	4th	5th
5	8	11	14	17

+ 3   +3   +3   +3

Each term is <u>3 more</u> than the one before it. That means that you need to start by <u>multiplying n by 3</u>.
Take the first term (where n = 1). If you multiply n by 3, you still have to <u>add 2</u> to get 5.
The same goes for n = 2. To get 8 you need to multiply n by 3, then add 2.
Every term in the sequence is worked out exactly the same way.

So the nth term is $3n + 2$

You can define a sequence by a Recurrence Relation too

Don't be put off by the fancy name — recurrence relations are pretty <u>easy</u> really.

The main thing to remember is:
x_n just means the nth term of the sequence

The <u>next term</u> in the sequence is x_{n+1}. You need to describe how to <u>work out</u> x_{n+1} if you're given x_n.
What you're actually doing is working out x_{n+1} as a <u>function</u> of x_n, so you can write $x_{n+1} = f(x_n)$.

Example: Find the recurrence relation of the sequence 5, 8, 11, 14, 17, ...

From the example above, you know that each term equals the one before it, plus 3.

This is written like this: $x_{n+1} = x_n + 3$

<u>BUT</u> $x_{n+1} = x_n + 3$ on its own <u>isn't enough</u> to describe 5, 8, 11, 14, 17,...
For example, the sequence 87, 90, 93, 96, 99, ... <u>also</u> has each term being 3 more than the one before.

The recurrence relation needs to be more <u>specific</u>, so you've got to <u>give one term</u> in the sequence.
You almost always give the <u>first value</u>, x_1.

Putting all of this together gives 5, 8, 11, 14, 17,... as $x_{n+1} = x_n + 3$, $x_1 = 5$

Like maths teachers, sequences can go on and on and on and on...

If you know the formula for the nth term, you can work out any term using a single formula, so it's kind of easy. If you only know a recurrence relation, then you can only work out the <u>next</u> term. So if you want the 20th term, and you only know the first one, then you have to use the recurrence relation 19 times. (So it'd be quicker to work out a formula really.)

Sequences

Some sequences involve *Multiplying*

You've done the easy 'adding' business. Now it gets really tough — <u>multiplying</u>. Are you sure you're ready for this?...

Example: A sequence is defined by $x_{n+1} = 2x_n - 1$, $x_2 = 5$. List the first five terms.

OK, you're told the second term, $x_2 = 5$. Just <u>plug that value</u> into the equation, and carry on from there.

$x_3 = 2 \times 5 - 1 = 9$ ⟵ *From the equation $x_n = x_2$ so $x_{n+1} = x_3$*

$x_4 = 2 \times 9 - 1 = 17$

$x_5 = 2 \times 17 - 1 = 33$ ⟵ *Now use x_3 to find $x_{n+1} = x_4$ and so on...*

Now to find the first term, a_1:

$x_2 = 2x_1 - 1$ ⟵ *Just make $x_n = x_1$*

$5 = 2x_1 - 1$

$2x_1 = 6$

$x_1 = 3$

So the first five terms of the sequence are 3, 5, 9, 17, 33 .

Some Sequences have a *Certain Number* of terms — others go on *Forever*

Some sequences are only defined for a <u>certain number</u> of terms.

For example, $x_{n+1} = x_n + 3$, $x_1 = 1$, $1 \le n \le 20$ will be 1, 4, 7, 10, ..., 58 and will contain 20 terms.
This is a finite sequence.

Other sequences <u>don't</u> have a specified number of terms and could go on <u>forever</u>.

For example, $u_{k+1} = u_k + 2$, $u_1 = 5$, will be 5, 7, 9, 11, 13, ... and won't have a final term.
This is an infinite sequence.

While others are <u>periodic</u>, and just revisit the same values over and over again.

For example, $u_k = u_{k-3}$, $u_1 = 1$, $u_2 = 4$, $u_3 = 2$, will be 1, 4, 2, 1, 4, 2, 1, 4, 2,...
This is a periodic sequence with period 3.

You can use *Recurrence Relations* to find the *Limit* of a sequence

Some sequences <u>tend to a limit</u> — the terms get <u>closer and closer</u> to a certain number (but don't necessarily ever reach it).

Example: A sequence has the recurrence relation $x_{n+1} = \frac{1}{2}x_n + 1$, and $x_1 = 1$.

So the terms of this sequence are: $x_1 = 1$, $x_2 = 1.5$, $x_3 = 1.75$, $x_4 = 1.875$, $x_5 = 1.9375$, $x_6 = 1.96875$, $x_7 = 1.984375$, etc.

1) The terms are getting closer and closer to 2.
   And even though no term will ever actually be equal to 2, the limit of the sequence is still 2.
2) This is written: $x_n \rightarrow 2$ as $n \rightarrow \infty$, and you say, "x_n *tends to 2 as n tends to infinity.*"

Not all sequences tend to a limit as $n \rightarrow \infty$ (e.g. the sequence 1, 2, 3, 4, 5... just gets bigger and bigger as $n \rightarrow \infty$).
But if a sequence does tend to a limit, you can find it by using the <u>recurrence relation</u>.

$$x_{n+1} = f(x_n)$$

Once the sequence reaches its limit (which it might not do until $x = \infty$), it <u>stays there</u>.
So to find the limit (often called L), you solve <u>$L = f(L)$</u>.

Example: To find the limit of the above sequence, you solve: <u>$L = \frac{1}{2}L + 1$</u>. ⟵ *The recurrence relation was $x_{n+1} = \frac{1}{2}x_n + 1$.*

i.e. $L - \frac{1}{2}L = 1$
i.e. $\frac{1}{2}L = 1$, and so <u>$L = 2$</u>, meaning the limit of the sequence is 2.

Arithmetic Progressions

Right, you've got basic sequences tucked under your belt now — time to step it up a notch (sounds painful).
When the terms of a sequence progress by <u>adding</u> a <u>fixed amount</u> each time, this is called an <u>arithmetic progression</u>.

It's all about *Finding* the nth *Term*

The <u>first term</u> of a sequence is given the symbol **a**. The <u>amount you add</u> each time is called the common difference, called **d**. The <u>position of any term</u> in the sequence is called **n**.

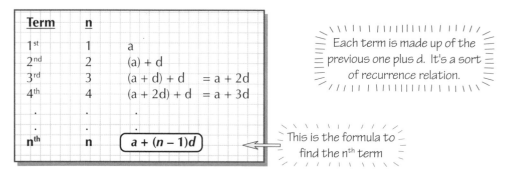

Term	n	
1st	1	a
2nd	2	$(a) + d$
3rd	3	$(a + d) + d \quad = a + 2d$
4th	4	$(a + 2d) + d \quad = a + 3d$
.	.	.
.	.	.
.	.	.
nth	n	$\boxed{a + (n - 1)d}$

Each term is made up of the previous one plus d. It's a sort of recurrence relation.

This is the formula to find the nth term

Example: Find the 20th term of the arithmetic progression 2, 5, 8, 11,... and find the formula for the nth term.

Here a = 2 and d = 3 ← *To get d, just find the difference between two terms next to each other — e.g. $11 - 8 = 3$*

So 20th term $= a + (20 - 1)d$
$= 2 + 19 \times 3$
$= 59$

The <u>general term</u> is the <u>nth term</u>, i.e. $a + (n - 1)d$
$= 2 + (n - 1)3$
$= 3n - 1$

A *Sequence* becomes a *Series* when you *Add the Terms* to Find the Total

S_n is the total of the first n terms of the arithmetic progression:

$$S_n = a + (a + d) + (a + 2d) + (a + 3d) + ... + (a + (n - 1)d)$$

There's a really neat version of the same formula too:

$$S_n = n \times \frac{(a + l)}{2}$$

The 'l' stands for the <u>last value</u> in the progression. You work it out as $l = a + (n - 1)d$

Nobody likes formulas, so think of it as the <u>average</u> of the <u>first and last</u> terms multiplied by the <u>number of terms</u>.

Example: Find the sum of the series with first term 3, last term 87 and common difference 4.

Here you know a, d and l, but you don't know n yet.

Use the information about the last value, l: $\quad a + (n - 1)d = 87$
Then <u>plug in</u> the other values: $\quad 3 + 4(n - 1) = 87$
$4n - 4 = 84$
$4n = 88$
$n = 22$

So $S_{22} = 22 \times \dfrac{(3 + 87)}{2}$ $\qquad S_{22} = 990$

Arithmetic Progressions

It's not always that simple though.
Should've done English, should've done English, should've done English, should've done English, should've done English...

They **Won't** always give you the **Last Term**...

...but don't panic — there's a formula to use when the <u>last term is unknown</u>. But you knew I'd say that, didn't you?

You know $l = a + (n - 1)d$ and $S_n = n\dfrac{(a+l)}{2}$.

Plug l into S_n and rearrange to get the formula in the box:

$$S_n = \frac{n}{2}[2a + (n-1)d]$$

Example: For the sequence -5, -2, 1, 4, 7, ... find the sum of the first 20 terms.

So $a = -5$ and $d = 3$. The question says $n = 20$ too.

$$S_{20} = \frac{20}{2}[2 \times -5 + (20 - 1) \times 3]$$
$$= 10\,[-10 + 19 \times 3]$$
$$S_{20} = 470$$

There's **Another** way of **Writing Series**, too

So far, the letter S has been used for the sum. The Greeks did a lot of work on this — their capital letter for S is <u>sigma</u>, or Σ. This is used today, together with the general term, to mean the <u>sum</u> of the series.

Example:

...and ending with n=15

Find $\displaystyle\sum_{n=1}^{15}(2n+3)$

Starting with n=1...

This means you have to find the sum of the <u>first 15 terms</u> of the series with n^{th} term $2n + 3$.

The first term ($n = 1$) is 5, the second term ($n = 2$) is 7, the third is 9, ... and the last term ($n = 15$) is 33. In other words, you need to find $5 + 7 + 9 + ... + 33$. This gives $a = 5$, $d = 2$, $n = 15$ and $l = 33$.

You know all of a, d, n and l, so you can use either formula:

$$S_n = n\frac{(a+l)}{2}$$
$$S_{15} = 15\frac{(5+33)}{2}$$
$$S_{15} = 15 \times 19$$
$$S_{15} = 285$$

It makes no difference which method you use.

$$S_n = \frac{n}{2}[2a + (n-1)d]$$
$$S_{15} = \frac{15}{2}[2 \times 5 + 14 \times 2]$$
$$S_{15} = \frac{15}{2}[10 + 28]$$
$$S_{15} = 285$$

This sigma notation is all Greek to me... *(Ho ho ho)*

A <u>sequence</u> is just a list of numbers (with commas between them) — a <u>series</u> on the other hand is when you add all the terms together. It doesn't sound like a big difference, but mathematicians get all hot under the collar when you get the two mixed up. Remember that Black<u>ADD</u>er was a great TV <u>series</u> — not a TV sequence. (Sounds daft, but I bet you remember it now.)

Arithmetic Progressions

Use *Arithmetic Progressions* to add up the *First n Whole Numbers*

The <u>sum of the first n natural numbers</u> looks like this: $S_n = 1 + 2 + 3 + \ldots + (n-2) + (n-1) + n$

So a = 1, l = n and also n = n. Now just plug those values into the formula:

Natural numbers are just positive whole numbers.

$$S_n = n \times \frac{(a+l)}{2} \implies \boxed{S_n = \frac{1}{2}n(n+1)}$$

Example: Add up all the whole numbers from 1 to 100.

Sounds pretty hard, but all you have to do is stick it into the formula:

$S_{100} = \frac{1}{2} \times 100 \times 101$. So $S_{100} = 5050$

Series *Don't* have to start with *n = 1*

Instead of adding up numbers from 1 to 100, you can add the natural numbers from, say, 50 to 100.
This just means the sum from 1 to 100, but <u>without</u> the first 49 whole numbers.

You can write this as
$$\sum_{n=50}^{100} n = \sum_{n=1}^{100} n - \sum_{n=1}^{49} n$$

Using $S_n = \frac{n(n+1)}{2}$

$$= 5050 - \frac{49 \times 50}{2}$$

From the example above.

$$= 5050 - 1225$$

$$= 3825$$

Subtract any *Series* if it *Doesn't* Start at *n = 1*

Example: Find $\displaystyle\sum_{n=7}^{20}(4n-1)$

$$\sum_{n=7}^{20}(4n-1) = \sum_{n=1}^{20}(4n-1) - \sum_{n=1}^{6}(4n-1)$$

Using $S_n = n\frac{(a+l)}{2}$

$$= \frac{20(3+79)}{2} - \frac{6(3+23)}{2}$$

$$= 820 - 78$$

$$= 742$$

NB: $\displaystyle\sum_{n=1}^{20}(4n-1)$ and $\displaystyle\sum_{n=1}^{6}(4n-1)$ could both have been worked out a different way:

$$\sum_{n=1}^{6}(4n-1) = \sum_{n=1}^{6}4n - \sum_{n=1}^{6}1$$

Because $\displaystyle\sum_{n=1}^{6}4n = 4\sum_{n=1}^{6}n$

$$= 4\sum_{n=1}^{6}n - \sum_{n=1}^{6}1$$

$\displaystyle\sum_{n=1}^{6}1 = 1+1+1+1+1+1 = 6$

$$= 4\left(\frac{6 \times 7}{2}\right) - 6$$

$$= 78$$

Geometric Progressions

So <u>arithmetic progressions</u> mean you <u>add</u> a number to get the next term.
<u>Geometric progressions</u> are a bit different — you <u>multiply</u> by a number to get the next term.

Geometric Progressions Multiply by a *Constant* each time

Geometric progressions work like this: the next term in the sequence is obtained by <u>multiplying the previous</u> one by a <u>constant value</u>. Couldn't be easier.

$$u_1 = a \qquad\qquad\qquad = a$$
$$u_2 = a \times r \qquad\qquad = ar$$
$$u_3 = a \times r \times r \qquad = ar^2$$
$$u_4 = a \times r \times r \times r = ar^3$$

The first term (u_1) is called 'a'.

The number you multiply by each time is called 'the common ratio', symbolised by 'r'.

Here's the formula describing any term in the geometric progression:

$$u_n = ar^{n-1}$$

Example: There is a chessboard with a 1p piece on the first square, 2p on the second square, 4p on the third, 8p on the forth and so on until the board is full. Calculate <u>how much money</u> is on the board.

This is a <u>geometric progression</u>, where you get the next term in the sequence by multiplying the previous one by 2.

So a = 1 (because you start with 1p on the first square) and r = 2.

So $u_1 = 1, u_2 = 2, u_3 = 4, u_4 = 8, ...$

You often have to work out the *Sum* of the *Terms*

Just like before, S_n stands for the <u>sum</u> of the <u>first n terms</u>.
In the example above, you're told to work out S_{64} (because there are 64 squares on a chessboard).

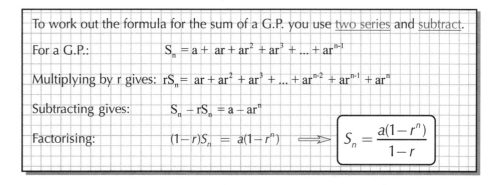

To work out the formula for the sum of a G.P. you use <u>two series</u> and <u>subtract</u>.

For a G.P.: $\qquad\qquad\qquad S_n = a + ar + ar^2 + ar^3 + ... + ar^{n-1}$

Multiplying by r gives: $\quad rS_n = ar + ar^2 + ar^3 + ... + ar^{n-2} + ar^{n-1} + ar^n$

Subtracting gives: $\qquad\quad S_n - rS_n = a - ar^n$

Factorising: $\qquad\qquad\quad (1-r)S_n = a(1-r^n) \implies \boxed{S_n = \dfrac{a(1-r^n)}{1-r}}$

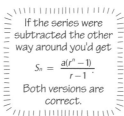

If the series were subtracted the other way around you'd get

$$S_n = \frac{a(r^n - 1)}{r - 1}.$$

Both versions are correct.

So, back to the chessboard example: $\quad a = 1, r = 2, n = 64 \qquad S_{64} = \dfrac{1(1-2^{64})}{1-2}$

$$S_{64} = 1.84 \times 10^{19} \text{ pence or } £1.84 \times 10^{17}$$

The whole is more than the sum of the parts — hmm, not in maths, it ain't...

You really need to understand the difference between arithmetic and geometric progressions — it's not hard, but it needs to be fixed firmly in your head. There are only a few formulas for sequences and series (the nth term of a sequence, the sum of the first n terms of a series), but you need to learn them, since they won't be in the formula book they give you.

Geometric Progressions

Geometric progressions can either Grow or Shrink

In the chessboard example, each term was <u>bigger</u> than the previous one, 1, 2, 4, 8, 16, …
You can create a series where each term is <u>less</u> than the previous one by using a <u>small value of r</u>.

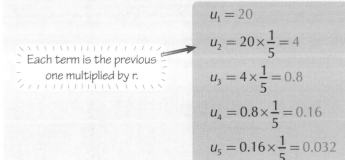

Example: If $a = 20$ and $r = \dfrac{1}{5}$, write down the first five terms of the sequence and the 20th term.

$$u_1 = 20$$
$$u_2 = 20 \times \frac{1}{5} = 4$$
$$u_3 = 4 \times \frac{1}{5} = 0.8$$
$$u_4 = 0.8 \times \frac{1}{5} = 0.16$$
$$u_5 = 0.16 \times \frac{1}{5} = 0.032$$

Each term is the previous one multiplied by r.

$$u_{20} = ar^{19}$$
$$= 20 \times \left(\frac{1}{5}\right)^{19}$$
$$= 1.048576 \times 10^{-12}$$

The sequence is <u>tending towards zero</u>, but won't ever get there.

In general, for each term to be <u>smaller</u> than the one before, you need $|r| < 1$. ⟵ *$|r|$ means the modulus (or size) of r, <u>ignoring the sign</u> of the number. So $|r| < 1$ means that $-1 < r < 1$.*
A sequence with $|r| < 1$ is called <u>convergent</u>, since the terms converge to a limit.
Any other sequence (like the chessboard example on page 25) is called <u>divergent</u>.

A Convergent series has a Sum to Infinity

In other words, if you just <u>kept</u> adding terms to a <u>convergent</u> series, you'd get <u>closer and closer</u> to a certain number, but you'd never actually reach it.

If $|r| < 1$ and n is very, very <u>big</u>, then r^n will be very, very <u>small</u> — or to put it technically, $r^n \to 0$. (Try working out $(\frac{1}{2})^{100}$ on your calculator if you don't believe me.)
This means $(1 - r^n)$ is really, really close to 1.

So, as $n \to \infty$, $S_n \to \dfrac{a}{1-r}$.

It's easier to remember as $\boxed{S_\infty = \dfrac{a}{1-r}}$

S_∞ just means 'sum to infinity'.

Example: If $a = 2$ and $r = \frac{1}{2}$, find the sum to infinity of the geometric series.

These values are getting <u>smaller</u> each time.

$$u_1 = 2 \qquad\longrightarrow\qquad S_1 = 2$$
$$u_2 = 2 \times \frac{1}{2} = 1 \qquad\longrightarrow\qquad S_2 = 2 + 1 = 3$$
$$u_3 = 1 \times \frac{1}{2} = \frac{1}{2} \qquad\longrightarrow\qquad S_3 = 2 + 1 + \frac{1}{2} = 3\frac{1}{2}$$
$$u_4 = \frac{1}{2} \times \frac{1}{2} = \frac{1}{4} \qquad\longrightarrow\qquad S_4 = 2 + 1 + \frac{1}{2} + \frac{1}{4} = 3\frac{3}{4}$$
$$u_5 = \frac{1}{4} \times \frac{1}{2} = \frac{1}{8} \qquad\longrightarrow\qquad S_5 = 2 + 1 + \frac{1}{2} + \frac{1}{4} + \frac{1}{8} = 3\frac{7}{8}$$
$$u_6 = \frac{1}{8} \times \frac{1}{2} = \frac{1}{16} \qquad\longrightarrow\qquad S_6 = 2 + 1 + \frac{1}{2} + \frac{1}{4} + \frac{1}{8} + \frac{1}{16} = 3\frac{15}{16}$$

These values are getting closer (<u>converging</u>) to 4.
So, the sum to infinity is 4.

You can show this <u>graphically</u>:
The line on the graph is getting <u>closer and closer</u> to 4, but it'll never actually get there.

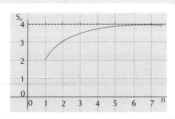

Of course, you could have saved yourself a lot of bother by using the <u>sum to infinity formula</u>:

$$S_\infty = \frac{a}{1-r} = \frac{2}{1-\frac{1}{2}} = 4$$

Geometric Progressions

Example: If $a = 2$ and $r = 2$, find the sum to infinity of the series.

$$u_1 = 2 \implies S_1 = 2$$
$$u_2 = 2 \times 2 = 4 \implies S_2 = 2 + 4 = 6$$
$$u_3 = 4 \times 2 = 8 \implies S_3 = 2 + 4 + 8 = 14$$
$$u_4 = 8 \times 2 = 16 \implies S_4 = 2 + 4 + 8 + 16 = 30$$
$$u_5 = 16 \times 2 = 32 \implies S_5 = 2 + 4 + 8 + 16 + 32 = 62$$

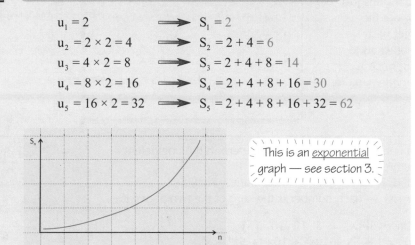

This is an <u>exponential</u> graph — see section 3.

As $n \to \infty$, $S_n \to \infty$ in a big way. So big, in fact, that eventually you <u>can't work it out</u> — so don't bother.

There is <u>no sum to infinity</u> for a <u>divergent</u> series.

Example: When a baby is born, £3000 is invested in an account with a fixed interest rate of 4% per year.
a) What will the account be worth at the start of the seventh year?
b) Will the account have doubled in value by the time the child reaches its 21st birthday?

a) $u_1 = a = 3000$

$u_2 = 3000 + (4\% \text{ of } 3000)$ ← This is the interest.

$\quad = 3000 + (0.04 \times 3000)$

$\quad = 3000 (1 + 0.04)$

$\quad = 3000 \times 1.04$ ← So, $r = 1.04$

$u_3 = u_2 \times 1.04$

$\quad = (3000 \times 1.04) \times 1.04$

$\quad = 3000 \times (1.04)^2$

$u_4 = 3000 \times (1.04)^3$

I've missed out some steps here — check that you understand what's happened.

. . .

. . .

$u_7 = 3000 \times (1.04)^6$

$\quad = £3795.96$ (to the nearest penny)

b) You need to know when $u_n > 6000$ ← double the original value.

From part a) you can tell that $u_n = 3000 \times (1.04)^{n-1}$

So $3000 \times (1.04)^{n-1} > 6000$

$(1.04)^{n-1} > 2$

To complete this you need to use logs (see section 3):

$\log(1.04)^{n-1} > \log 2$

$(n - 1) \log(1.04) > \log 2$

$$n - 1 > \frac{\log 2}{\log 1.04}$$

$n - 1 > 17.67$

$n > 18.67$ (to 2 d.p.)

So u_{19} (the amount at the start of the 19th year) will be more than double the original amount — plenty of time to buy a Porsche for the 21st birthday.

So tell me — if my savings earn 4% per year, when will I be rich...

Now here's a funny thing — you can have a convergent geometric series if the common ratio is small enough.
I find this odd — that I can keep adding things to a sum forever, but the sum never gets really really big.

Binomial Expansions

If you're feeling a bit stressed, just take a couple of minutes to relax before trying to get your head round this page — it's a bit of a stinker in places. Have a cup of tea and think about something else for a couple of minutes. Ready...

Writing *Binomial Expansions* is all about *Spotting Patterns*

Doing binomial expansions just involves <u>multiplying out</u> the brackets. It would get nasty when you raise the brackets to <u>higher powers</u> — but once again I've got a <u>cunning plan</u>...

$$(1+x)^0 = 1$$
$$(1+x)^1 = 1+x$$
$$(1+x)^2 = 1+2x+x^2$$
$$(1+x)^3 = 1+3x+3x^2+x^3$$
$$(1+x)^4 = 1+4x+6x^2+4x^3+x^4$$

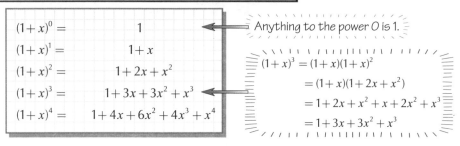

Anything to the power 0 is 1.

$$(1+x)^3 = (1+x)(1+x)^2$$
$$= (1+x)(1+2x+x^2)$$
$$= 1+2x+x^2+x+2x^2+x^3$$
$$= 1+3x+3x^2+x^3$$

A Frenchman named Pascal spotted the pattern in the coefficients and wrote them down in a <u>triangle</u>.
So it was called 'Pascal's Triangle' (imaginative, eh?).
The pattern's easy — each number is the <u>sum</u> of the two above it.

So, the next line will be: **1 5 10 10 5 1**
giving **(1 + x)⁵ = 1 + 5x + 10x² + 10x³ + 5x⁴ + x⁵.**

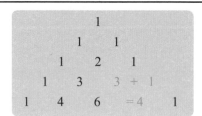

You *Don't* need to write out Pascal's Triangle for *Higher Powers*

There's a formula for the numbers in the triangle. The formula looks <u>horrible</u> (one of the worst in AS maths) so don't try to learn it letter by letter — look for the <u>patterns</u> in it instead. Here's an example:

Example: Expand $(1 + x)^{20}$, giving the first four terms only.

So you can use this formula for any power, the power is called n. In this example n = 20.

$$(1+x)^n = 1 + \frac{n}{1}x + \frac{n(n-1)}{1\times 2}x^2 + \boxed{\frac{n(n-1)(n-2)}{1\times 2\times 3}x^3} + \dots\dots + x^n$$

Here's a closer look at the term in the black box:

There are <u>three things</u> multiplied together on the top row. If n=20, this would be 20×19×18.

$$\frac{n(n-1)(n-2)}{1\times 2\times 3}x^3$$

<u>Start here</u>. The power of x is 3 and everything else here is based on 3.

There are <u>three integers</u> here multiplied together.
1×2×3 is written as 3! and called 3 <u>factorial</u>.

This means, if n = 20 and you were asked for '<u>the term in x⁷</u>' you should write $\dfrac{20\times 19\times 18\times 17\times 16\times 15\times 14}{1\times 2\times 3\times 4\times 5\times 6\times 7}x^7$.

This can be <u>simplified</u> to $\dfrac{20!}{7!13!}x^7$ ⟵ $20\times 19\times 18\times 17\times 16\times 15\times 14 = \dfrac{20!}{13!}$ because it's the numbers from 20 to 1 multiplied together, divided by the numbers from 13 to 1 multiplied together.

Believe it or not, there's an even <u>shorter</u> form: $\dfrac{20!}{7!13!}$ is written as $^{20}C_7$ or $\dbinom{20}{7}$

$$^nC_r = \binom{n}{r} = \frac{n!}{r!(n-r)!}$$

So, to finish the example, $(1+x)^{20} = 1 + \dfrac{20}{1}x + \dfrac{20\times 19}{1\times 2}x^2 + \dfrac{20\times 19\times 18}{1\times 2\times 3}x^3 + \dots$ $= 1 + 20x + 190x^2 + 1140x^3 + \dots$

Binomial Expansions

It's slightly more complicated when the Coefficient of x isn't 1

Example: What is the term in x^5 in the expansion of $(1 - 3x)^{12}$?

The term in x^5 will be as follows:

$$\frac{12 \times 11 \times 10 \times 9 \times 8}{1 \times 2 \times 3 \times 4 \times 5}(-3x)^5$$

Watch out — the –3 is included here with the x.

$$= \frac{12!}{5!7!}(-3)^5 x^5 \quad = -\frac{12!}{5!7!} \times 3^5 x^5 = -192456x^5$$

Note that $(-3)^{even}$ will always be <u>positive</u> and $(-3)^{odd}$ will always be <u>negative</u>.

Here's another tip — the digits on the <u>bottom</u> of the fraction should always <u>add up</u> to the number on the <u>top</u>.

Some Binomials contain More Complicated Expressions

The binomials so far have all had a <u>1</u> in the brackets — things get tricky when there's a <u>number other than 1</u>. Don't panic, though. The method is the same as before once you've done a bit of <u>factorising</u>.

Example: What is the coefficient of x^4 in the expansion of $(2 + 5x)^7$?

Factorising $(2 + 5x)$ gives $2(1 + \frac{5}{2}x)$

So, $(2 + 5x)^7$ gives $2^7(1 + \frac{5}{2}x)^7$

It's really easy to forget the first bit (here it's 2^7) — you've been warned...

$$(2 + 5x)^7 = 2^7(1 + \frac{5}{2}x)^7$$

$$= 2^7[1 + 7\left(\frac{5}{2}x\right) + \frac{7 \times 6}{1 \times 2}\left(\frac{5}{2}x\right)^2 + \frac{7 \times 6 \times 5}{1 \times 2 \times 3}\left(\frac{5}{2}x\right)^3 + \frac{7 \times 6 \times 5 \times 4}{1 \times 2 \times 3 \times 4}\left(\frac{5}{2}x\right)^4 + ...]$$

Here's the one you want.

The coefficient of x^4 will be $2^7 \times \frac{7!}{4!3!}(\frac{5}{2})^4 = 175000$

Don't forget the 2^7.

So, there's <u>no need</u> to work out all of the terms.

In fact, you could have gone <u>directly</u> to the term in x^4 by using the method on page 28.

> Note: The question asked for the <u>coefficient of x^4</u> in the expansion, so <u>don't include any x's</u> in your answer. If you'd been asked for the <u>term in x^4</u> in the expansion, then you <u>should</u> have included the x^4 in your answer.
>
> <u>Always</u> read the question very carefully.

Pascal was fine at maths but rubbish at music — he only played the triangle...

You can use your calculator to work out these tricky fractions — you use the ^nC_r button (though it could be called something else on your calculator). So to work out $^{20}C_7$, press '20', then press the ^nC_r button, then press '7', and then finish with '='. Now work out $^{15}C_7$ and $^{15}C_8$ — you should get the same answers, since they're both $\frac{15!}{7!8!}$.

Section Four Revision Questions

What's that I hear you cry? You want revision questions — and lots of them. Well it just so happens I've got a few here. Loads of questions on sequences, series and binomial expansions.

With sequences and series, get a clear idea in your head before you start, or you could get to the end of the question and realise the series is arithmetic, not geometric. That would be bad.

1) A sequence has an nth term of $n^2 + 3$. Find a) the first four terms, and b) the 20th term.

2) A sequence is defined by $x_{n+1} = 3x_n - 2$, $x_1 = 4$. Find x_2, x_3 and x_4.

3) The recurrence relation of a sequence is $x_{n+1} = \dfrac{3x_n}{4} + 7$. Find the limit as $n \to \infty$.

4) Find the sum of the arithmetic progression that begins with 5, 8, ... and ends with 65.

5) A series has 1st term 7 and 5th term 23. Find:
   a) the common difference,
   b) the 15th term,
   c) the sum of the first ten terms.

6) An arithmetic progression has seventh term 36 and tenth term 30.
   Find the sum of the first five terms and the nth term.

7) Find: a) $\displaystyle\sum_{n=1}^{20}(3n-1)$

   b) $\displaystyle\sum_{n=1}^{10}(48-5n)$.

8) For the sequence 2, –6, 18, ..., find the 10th term.

9) For the sequence 24, 12, 6, ..., find:
   a) the common ratio,
   b) the seventh term,
   c) the sum to infinity.

10) A geometric progression and an arithmetic progression both begin with 2, 6, ...
   Which term of the arithmetic progression will be equal to the fifth term of the geometric progression?

11) Find the coefficient of x^2 in the expansion of $(2 + 3x)^5$.

Integration

Integration is the 'opposite' of differentiation — and so if you can differentiate, you can be pretty confident you'll be able to integrate too. There's just one extra thing you have to remember — the constant of integration...

You need the constant because there's **More Than One** right answer

When you integrate something, you're trying to find a function that returns to what you started with when you differentiate it. And when you add the constant of integration, you're just allowing for the fact that there's <u>more</u> than one possible function that does this...

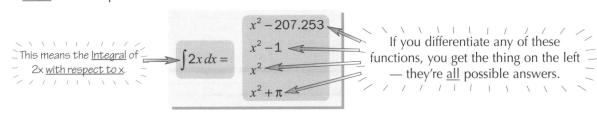

This means the <u>Integral</u> of 2x <u>with respect to x</u>.

$$\int 2x\,dx = \begin{array}{l} x^2 - 207.253 \\ x^2 - 1 \\ x^2 \\ x^2 + \pi \end{array}$$

If you differentiate any of these functions, you get the thing on the left — they're <u>all</u> possible answers.

So the answer to this integral is actually... $\int 2x\,dx = x^2 + C$

The 'C' just means 'any number'.
This is the <u>constant of integration</u>.

You only need to add a constant of integration to <u>indefinite integrals</u> — these are just integrals without <u>limits</u> (or little numbers) next to the integral sign. (If that doesn't make sense, you'll see what I mean later on.)

Up the power by **One** — then **Divide** by it

The formula below tells you how to integrate any power of x (except x^{-1}).

This is an indefinite integral — it doesn't have any limits (numbers) next to the integral sign.

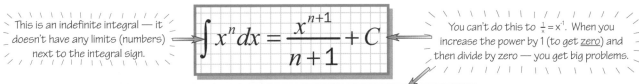

$$\int x^n\,dx = \frac{x^{n+1}}{n+1} + C$$

You can't do this to $\frac{1}{x} = x^{-1}$. When you increase the power by 1 (to get <u>zero</u>) and then divide by zero — you get big problems.

In a nutshell, this says:

> To integrate a power of x: (i) Increase the power by one — then divide by it.
> and (ii) Stick a constant on the end.

EXAMPLES: Use the integration formula...

① For '<u>normal</u>' powers,

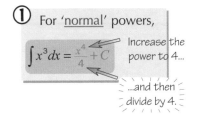

$$\int x^3\,dx = \frac{x^4}{4} + C$$

Increase the power to 4...
...and then divide by 4.

② For <u>negative</u> powers,

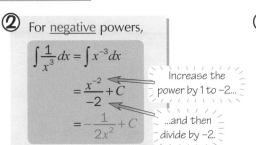

$$\int \frac{1}{x^3}\,dx = \int x^{-3}\,dx$$
$$= \frac{x^{-2}}{-2} + C$$
$$= -\frac{1}{2x^2} + C$$

Increase the power by 1 to −2...
...and then divide by −2.

③ For <u>fractional</u> powers,

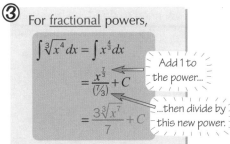

$$\int \sqrt[3]{x^4}\,dx = \int x^{\frac{4}{3}}\,dx$$
$$= \frac{x^{\frac{7}{3}}}{(\frac{7}{3})} + C$$
$$= \frac{3\sqrt[3]{x^7}}{7} + C$$

Add 1 to the power...
...then divide by this new power.

④ And for complicated looking stuff...

$$\int \left(3x^2 - \frac{2}{\sqrt{x}} + \frac{7}{x^2}\right)dx = \int \left(3x^2 - 2x^{-\frac{1}{2}} + 7x^{-2}\right)dx$$
$$= \frac{3x^3}{3} - \frac{2x^{\frac{1}{2}}}{(\frac{1}{2})} + \frac{7x^{-1}}{-1} + C$$
$$= x^3 - 4\sqrt{x} - \frac{7}{x} + C$$

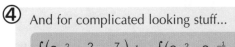

Do each of these bits separately.

CHECK YOUR ANSWERS:
You can check you've integrated properly by <u>differentiating</u> the <u>answer</u> — you should end up with the thing you started with.

Indefinite integrals — joy without limits...

This integration lark isn't so bad then — there's only a couple of things to remember and then you can do it no problem. But that constant of integration catches loads of people out — it's so easy to forget — and you'll definitely lose marks if you do forget it. You have been warned. Other than that, there's not much to it. Hurray.

Integration

By now, you're probably aware that maths isn't something you do unless you're a bit of a <u>thrill-seeker</u>.
You know, sometimes they even ask you to find a curve with a certain derivative that goes through a certain point.

You sometimes need to find the Value of the Constant of Integration

When they tell you something else about the curve in addition to its derivative, you can work out the value of that <u>constant of integration</u>. Usually the something is the <u>coordinates</u> of one of the points the curve goes through.

Really Important Bit...

When you differentiate y, you get $\frac{dy}{dx}$.

And when you integrate $\frac{dy}{dx}$, you get y*.

$$y \xrightarrow{\text{Differentiate}} \frac{dy}{dx}$$
$$y \xleftarrow{\text{Integrate}} \frac{dy}{dx}$$

*If you ignore the constant of integration.

EXAMPLE: Find the equation of the curve through the point (2, 8) with $\frac{dy}{dx} = 6x(x-1)$.

You know the derivative and need to find the function — so <u>integrate</u>.

Remember:
Even if you <u>don't</u> have any extra information about the curve — you still have to add a <u>constant</u> when you work out an integral <u>without limits</u>.

$$\frac{dy}{dx} = 6x(x-1) = 6x^2 - 6x$$

So integrating both sides gives...

$$y = \int (6x^2 - 6x)\,dx$$

$$\Rightarrow y = \frac{6x^3}{3} - \frac{6x^2}{2} + C$$

Don't forget the constant of integration.

$$\Rightarrow y = 2x^3 - 3x^2 + C$$

Check this is correct by differentiating it and making sure you get what you started with.

$$y = 2x^3 - 3x^2 + C = 2x^3 - 3x^2 + Cx^0$$

$$\Rightarrow \frac{dy}{dx} = 2(3x^2) - 3(2x^1) + C(0x^{-1})$$

$$\Rightarrow \frac{dy}{dx} = 6x^2 - 6x$$

So this function's got the correct derivative — but you haven't finished yet.

You now need to <u>find C</u> — and you do this by using the fact that it goes through the point (2, 8).

$$y = 2x^3 - 3x^2 + C$$

Putting x = 2 and y = 8 in the above equation gives...

$$8 = (2 \times 2^3) - (3 \times 2^2) + C$$

$$\Rightarrow 8 = 16 - 12 + C$$

$$\Rightarrow C = 4$$

So the answer you need is this one:

$$y = 2x^3 - 3x^2 + 4$$

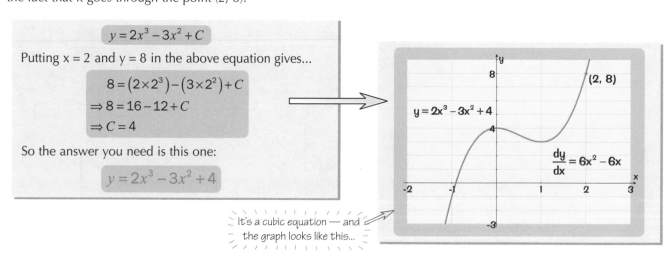

It's a cubic equation — and the graph looks like this...

Maths and alcohol don't mix — so never drink and derive...

That's another page under your belt and — go on, admit it — there was nothing too horrendous on it. If you can do the stuff from the previous page and then substitute some numbers into an equation, you can do everything from this page too. So if you think this is boring, you'd be right. But if you think it's much harder than the stuff before, you'd be wrong.

Integration

Some integrals have <u>limits</u> (i.e. little numbers) next to the integral sign. You integrate them in exactly the same way — but you <u>don't</u> need a constant of integration. Much easier. And scrummier and yummier too.

A *Definite Integral* finds the *Area Under a Curve*

This definite integral tells you the <u>area</u> between the graph of $y = x^3$ and the x-axis between $x = -2$ and $x = 2$:

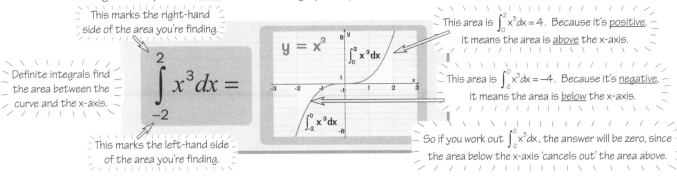

This marks the right-hand side of the area you're finding.

Definite integrals find the area between the curve and the x-axis.

$$\int_{-2}^{2} x^3\, dx =$$

This marks the left-hand side of the area you're finding.

This area is $\int_{0}^{2} x^3 dx = 4$. Because it's <u>positive</u>, it means the area is <u>above</u> the x-axis.

This area is $\int_{-2}^{0} x^3 dx = -4$. Because it's <u>negative</u>, it means the area is <u>below</u> the x-axis.

So if you work out $\int_{-2}^{2} x^3 dx$, the answer will be zero, since the area below the x-axis 'cancels out' the area above.

Do the integration in the same way — then use the *Limits*

Finding a definite integral isn't really any harder than an indefinite one — there's just an <u>extra</u> stage you have to do. After you've integrated the function you have to work out the value of this new function by sticking in the <u>limits</u>.

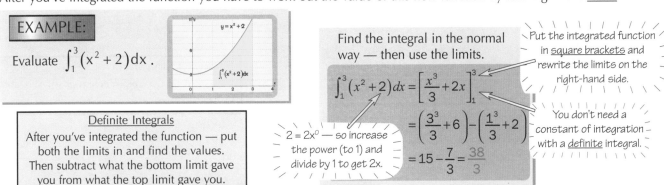

EXAMPLE:

Evaluate $\int_{1}^{3}(x^2 + 2)\,dx$.

Find the integral in the normal way — then use the limits.

$$\int_{1}^{3}(x^2+2)\,dx = \left[\frac{x^3}{3} + 2x\right]_{1}^{3}$$

$$= \left(\frac{3^3}{3} + 6\right) - \left(\frac{1^3}{3} + 2\right)$$

$$= 15 - \frac{7}{3} = \frac{38}{3}$$

$2 = 2x^0$ — so increase the power (to 1) and divide by 1 to get 2x.

Put the integrated function in <u>square brackets</u> and rewrite the limits on the right-hand side.

You don't need a constant of integration with a <u>definite</u> integral.

Definite Integrals
After you've integrated the function — put both the limits in and find the values. Then subtract what the bottom limit gave you from what the top limit gave you.

Integrate 'to Infinity' with the ∞ (infinity) sign

And you can integrate all the way to <u>infinity</u> as well. Just use the ∞ symbol as your upper limit. Or use $-∞$ as your lower limit if you want to integrate to 'minus infinity'.

EXAMPLE: Find the area under the curve $y = \frac{15}{x^2} - \frac{30}{x^3}$ for $x \geq 2$.

$$A = \int_{2}^{\infty}\left(\frac{15}{x^2} - \frac{30}{x^3}\right) = 15\int_{2}^{\infty}(x^{-2} - 2x^{-3})\,dx$$

$$= 15\left[\frac{x^{-1}}{-1} - \frac{2x^{-2}}{(-2)}\right]_{2}^{\infty}$$

$$= 15\left[-\frac{1}{x} + \frac{1}{x^2}\right]_{2}^{\infty}$$

$$= 15\left\{(-0+0) - \left(-\frac{1}{2} + \frac{1}{4}\right)\right\} = 15 \times \frac{1}{4} = \frac{15}{4}$$

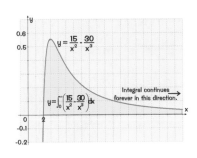

My hobbies? Well I'm really inte grating. Especially carrots.

It's still integration — but this time you're putting two numbers into an equation afterwards. So although this may not be the wild and crazy fun-packed time your teachers promised you when they were trying to persuade you to take AS maths, you've got to admit that a lot of this stuff is pretty similar — and if you can do one bit, you can use that to do quite a few other bits too. Maths is like that. But I admit it's probably not as much fun as a big banana-and-toffee cake.

Areas Between Curves

With a bit of thought, you can use integration to find all kinds of areas — even ones that look quite tricky at first. The best way to work out what to do is draw a <u>picture</u>. Then it'll seem easier. I promise you it will.

Sometimes you have to **Add** integrals...

This looks pretty hard — until you draw a picture and see what it's all about.

EXAMPLE: Find the area enclosed by the curves $y = x^2$, $y = (2 - x)^2$ and the x-axis.

Find out where the curves meet by <u>solving</u> $x^2 = (2-x)^2$. — they meet at x=1.

You have to find area A — but you'll need to <u>split</u> it into two smaller pieces.

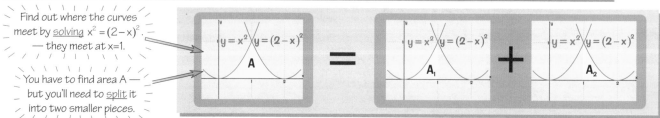

And it's pretty clear from the picture that you'll have to find the area in two lumps, A_1 and A_2.

The first area you need to find is A_1:

$$A_1 = \int_0^1 x^2\, dx$$
$$= \left[\frac{x^3}{3}\right]_0^1$$
$$= \left(\frac{1}{3} - 0\right) = \frac{1}{3}$$

The other area you need is A_2:

$$A_2 = \int_1^2 (2-x)^2\, dx = \int_1^2 \left(4 - 4x + x^2\right) dx$$
$$= \left[4x - 2x^2 + \frac{x^3}{3}\right]_1^2$$
$$= \left(8 - 8 + \frac{8}{3}\right) - \left(4 - 2 + \frac{1}{3}\right)$$
$$= \frac{8}{3} - \frac{7}{3} = \frac{1}{3}$$

And the area the question actually asks for is $A_1 + A_2$. This is

$$A = A_1 + A_2$$
$$= \frac{1}{3} + \frac{1}{3} = \frac{2}{3}$$

If you spot that the area A is <u>symmetrical</u> about x = 1, you can save yourself some work by calculating half the area and then doubling it: $A = 2\int_0^1 x^2\, dx$

...sometimes you have to **Subtract** them

Again, it's best to look at the <u>pictures</u> to work out exactly what you need to do.

EXAMPLE: Find the area enclosed by the curves $y = x^2 + 1$ and $y = 9 - x^2$.

Solve $x^2 + 1 = 9 - x^2$ to find where the curves meet.
$x^2 + 1 = 9 - x^2 \Rightarrow 2x^2 = 8$
$\Rightarrow x^2 = 4$
$\Rightarrow x = \pm 2$

So you'll have to integrate between −2 and 2.

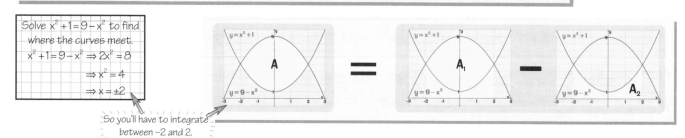

The area under the green curve A_1 is:

$$A_1 = \int_{-2}^2 \left(9 - x^2\right) dx$$
$$= \left[9x - \frac{x^3}{3}\right]_{-2}^2$$
$$= \left(18 - \frac{2^3}{3}\right) - \left(-18 - \frac{(-2)^3}{3}\right)$$
$$= \left(18 - \frac{8}{3}\right) - \left(-18 - \left(-\frac{8}{3}\right)\right) = \frac{46}{3} - \left(-\frac{46}{3}\right) = \frac{92}{3}$$

The area under the red curve is:

$$A_2 = \int_{-2}^2 \left(x^2 + 1\right) dx$$
$$= \left[\frac{x^3}{3} + x\right]_{-2}^2$$
$$= \left(\frac{2^3}{3} + 2\right) - \left(\frac{(-2)^3}{3} + (-2)\right)$$
$$= \left(\frac{8}{3} + 2\right) - \left(-\frac{8}{3} - 2\right) = \frac{28}{3}$$

And the area you need is the difference between these:

$$A = A_1 - A_2$$
$$= \frac{92}{3} - \frac{28}{3} = \frac{64}{3}$$

Instead of integrating before subtracting — you could try 'subtracting the lines', and then integrating. This last area A is also:

$$A = \int_{-2}^2 \left\{\left(9 - x^2\right) - \left(x^2 + 1\right)\right\} dx$$

And so, our hero integrates the area between two curves, and saves the day...

That's the basic idea of finding the area enclosed by two curves and lines — draw a picture and then break the area down into smaller, easier chunks. And it's always a good idea to keep an eye out for anything symmetrical that could save you a bit of work — like in the first example. Questions like this aren't hard — but they can sometimes take a long time. Great.

The Trapezium Rule

Sometimes <u>integrals</u> can be just <u>too hard</u> to do using the normal methods — then you need to know other ways to solve them. That's where the <u>Trapezium Rule</u> comes in.

The *Trapezium Rule* is Used to Find the *Approximate Area* Under a Curve

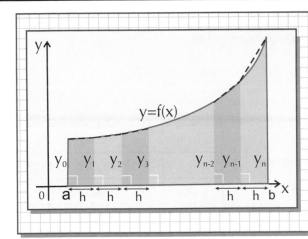

The area represented by $\int_a^b y\,dx$ is approximately:

$$\int_a^b y\,dx \approx \frac{h}{2}[y_0 + 2(y_1 + y_2 + ... + y_{n-1}) + y_n]$$

where **n** is the number of strips or intervals and **h** is the width of each strip.

You can find the width of each strip using $h = \frac{(b-a)}{n}$

$y_0, y_1, y_2, ... , y_n$ are the heights of the sides of the trapeziums — you get these by putting the x-values into the curve.

So basically the formula for approximating $\int_a^b y\,dx$ works like this:

'Add the first and last heights $(y_0 + y_n)$ and add this to <u>twice</u> all the other heights added up — then multiply by $\frac{h}{2}$.'

Example: Find an approximate value for $\int_0^2 \sqrt{4 - x^2}\,dx$ using 4 strips. Give your answer to 4 s.f.

Start by working out the width of each strip: $h = \frac{(b-a)}{n} = \frac{(2-0)}{4} = 0.5$

This means the x-values are $x_0 = 0$, $x_1 = 0.5$, $x_2 = 1$, $x_3 = 1.5$ and $x_4 = 2$ (the question specifies 4 strips, so n = 4). Set up a table and work out the y-values or heights using the equation in the integral.

x	$y = \sqrt{4 - x^2}$
$x_0 = 0$	$y_0 = \sqrt{4 - 0^2} = 2$
$x_1 = 0.5$	$y_1 = \sqrt{4 - 0.5^2} = \sqrt{3.75} = 1.936491673$
$x_2 = 1.0$	$y_2 = \sqrt{4 - 1.0^2} = \sqrt{3} = 1.732050808$
$x_3 = 1.5$	$y_3 = \sqrt{4 - 1.5^2} = \sqrt{1.75} = 1.322875656$
$x_4 = 2.0$	$y_4 = \sqrt{4 - 2.0^2} = 0$

Now put all the y-values into the formula with h and n:

$$\int_a^b y\,dx \approx \frac{0.5}{2}[2 + 2(1.936491673 + 1.732050808 + 1.322875656) + 0]$$
$$\approx 0.25[2 + 2 \times 4.991418137]$$
$$\approx 2.996 \text{ to 4 s.f.}$$

Watch out — if they ask you to work out a question with 5 y-values (or '<u>ordinates</u>') then this is the <u>same</u> as 4 strips. The x-values usually go up in <u>nice jumps</u> — if they don't then <u>check</u> your calculations carefully.

The *Approximation* might be an *Overestimate* or an *Underestimate*

It all depends on the shape of the curve...

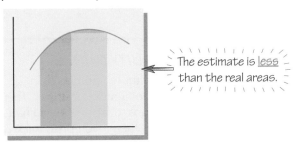

The estimate is <u>less</u> than the real areas.

The estimate is <u>more</u> than the real areas.

The Trapezium Rule

These are usually popular questions with examiners — as long as you're careful there are <u>plenty of marks</u> to be had.

The **Trapezium Rule** is in the **Formula Booklet**

...so don't try any heroics — always <u>look it up</u> and use it with these questions.

Example: Use the trapezium rule with 7 ordinates to find an approximation to $\int_{1}^{2.2} 2\log_{10} x \, dx$

Remember, <u>7 ordinates</u> means <u>6 strips</u> — so n = 6.

Calculate the width of the strips: $h = \dfrac{(b-a)}{n} = \dfrac{(2.2-1)}{6} = 0.2$

Set up a table and work out the y-values using $y = 2\log_{10} x$: ⟶

x	$y = 2\log_{10} x$
$x_0 = 1.0$	$y_0 = 2\log_{10} 1 = 0$
$x_1 = 1.2$	$y_1 = 2\log_{10} 1.2 = 0.15836$
$x_2 = 1.4$	$y_2 = 0.29226$
$x_3 = 1.6$	$y_3 = 0.40824$
$x_4 = 1.8$	$y_4 = 0.51055$
$x_5 = 2.0$	$y_5 = 0.60206$
$x_6 = 2.2$	$y_6 = 0.68485$

Putting all these values in the formula gives: $\quad y_6 = 2\log_{10} b = 0.68485$

$$\int_{a}^{b} y\,dx \approx \frac{0.2}{2}[0 + 2(0.15836 + 0.29226 + 0.40824 + 0.51055 + 0.60206) + 0.68485]$$

$$\approx 0.1 \times [0.68485 + 2 \times 1.97147]$$

$$\approx 0.462779$$

$$\approx 0.463 \text{ to 3 d.p.}$$

Example: Use the trapezium rule with 8 intervals to find an approximation to $\int_{0}^{\pi} \sin x \, dx$

Whenever you get a calculus question using <u>trig functions</u>, you <u>have</u> to use <u>radians</u>. You'll probably be given a limit with π in, which is a pretty good reminder.

There are 8 intervals, so n = 8.

$\quad$ Keep your x-values in terms of π.

Calculate the width of the strips: $h = \dfrac{(b-a)}{n} = \dfrac{(\pi-0)}{8} = \dfrac{\pi}{8}$

Set up a table and work out the y-values: ⟶

So, putting all this in the formula gives:

x	$y = \sin x$
$x_0 = 0$	$y_0 = \sin 0 = 0$
$x_1 = \dfrac{\pi}{8}$	$y_1 = 0.38268$
$x_2 = \dfrac{\pi}{4}$	$y_2 = 0.70711$
$x_3 = \dfrac{3\pi}{8}$	$y_3 = 0.92388$
$x_4 = \dfrac{\pi}{2}$	$y_4 = 1$
$x_5 = \dfrac{5\pi}{8}$	$y_5 = 0.92388$
$x_6 = \dfrac{3\pi}{4}$	$y_6 = 0.70711$
$x_7 = \dfrac{7\pi}{8}$	$y_7 = 0.38268$
$x_8 = \pi$	$y_8 = 0$

$$\int_{a}^{b} y\,dx \approx \frac{1}{2}\cdot\frac{\pi}{8}[0 + 2(0.38268 + 0.70711 + 0.92388 + 1 + 0.92388 + 0.70711 + 0.38268) + 0]$$

$$\approx \frac{\pi}{16}[2 \times 5.02734]$$

$$\approx 1.9742$$

$$\approx 1.974 \text{ to 3 d.p.}$$

Maths rhyming slang #3: Dribble and drool — Trapezium rule...

Take your time with Trapezium Rule questions — it's so easy to make a mistake with all those numbers flying around. Make a nice table showing all your ordinates (careful — this is always one more than the number of strips). Then add up y_1 to y_{n-1} and multiply the answer by 2. Add on y_0 and y_n. Finally, multiply what you've got so far by the width of a strip and <u>divide by 2</u>. It's a good idea to write down what you get after each stage, by the way — then if you press the wrong button (easily done) you'll be able to pick up from where you went wrong. They're not hard — just fiddly.

Section Five Revision Questions

That's what integration's all about. And really, if you can differentiate, you can integrate too.
Yes, there are fiddly things to remember — like that constant of integration, for one — but overall, there are worse things you'll have to do. And just think of all the lovely marks you'll get if you can answer questions like these in the exam...

1) Write down the steps involved in integrating a power of x. What's the only power of x that these rules don't work for? (Come on, come on — you need to know.)

2) What's an indefinite integral? Why do you have to add a constant of integration when you find an indefinite integral?

3) How can you check whether you've integrated something properly? (Without asking someone else.)

4) Integrate these: a) $\int 10x^4 dx$, b) $\int \frac{4}{x^3} dx$, c) $\int (3x^3 + 2x^2) dx$, d) $\int 4\sqrt[3]{x} dx$, e) $\int \left(6x^5 - \frac{2}{x^2} + \sqrt{x}\right) dx$.
   (Massive yawn.)

5) Work out the equation of the curve that goes through the point (1, 0) and has derivative $\frac{dy}{dx} = 6x - 7$.

6) Find the equation of the curve that has derivative $\frac{dy}{dx} = \sqrt{x} + \frac{2}{x^2}$ and goes through the point (1, 0).

   How would you change the equation if the curve had to go through the point (1, 2) instead?
   (Don't start the whole question again.)

7) How can you tell whether an integral is a definite one or an indefinite one?
   (It's easy really — it just sounds difficult.)

8) What does a definite integral represent on a graph?

9) Evaluate: a) $\int_{-3}^{3} (9 - x^2) dx$, b) $\int_{1}^{\infty} \frac{3}{x^2} dx$. Sketch the areas represented by these integrals.

10) Evaluate these definite integrals: a) $\int_{0}^{1} (4x^3 + 3x^2 + 2x + 1) dx$, b) $\int_{1}^{2} \left(\frac{8}{x^5} + \frac{3}{\sqrt{x}}\right) dx$, c) $\int_{1}^{6} \frac{3}{x^2} dx$.

11) Find the yellow area in each of these graphs:

a)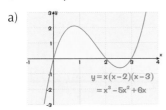
b)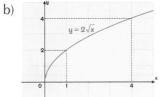
c)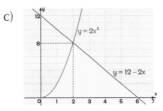
d)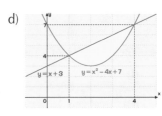

12) Use the trapezium rule with n intervals to estimate the following integrals (to 4 s.f.):

a) $\int_{0}^{3} (9 - x^2)^{\frac{1}{2}} dx$ with $n = 3$

b) $\int_{0.2}^{1.2} x^{x^2} dx$; $n = 5$

38

General Certificate of Education
Advanced Subsidiary (AS) and Advanced Level

Core 2 Mathematics — Practice Exam One

Give non-exact numerical answers correct to 3 significant figures, unless a
different degree of accuracy is specified in the question or is clearly appropriate.

1 (i) By sketching the graph of $y = \tan 2t$ for a suitable range of t, determine the number of solutions to
the equation $\tan 2t = k$ in the range $0° \le t < 360°$, where k is any number. [3]

(ii) Solve the equation $\sin 2t = \sqrt{2} \cos 2t$, giving all the solutions in the range $0° \le t < 360°$. [3]

2 (i) Write down the value of $\log_3 3$ [1]

(ii) Given that $\log_a \chi = \log_a 4 + 3 \log_a 2$ show that $\chi = 32$ [2]

3 (i) Sketch the curve $y = \dfrac{1}{x^2}$ for $x > 0$. [1]

(ii) Show that $\displaystyle\int_1^\infty \frac{1}{x^2}\,dx = 1$. [2]

(iii) Find the equation of f(x), where f(x) is the tangent to the graph of $y = \dfrac{1}{x^2}$ at the point where $x = 1$. [2]

(iv) Find k < 1 such that $\displaystyle\int_0^k f(x)\,dx = 1$. Give your answer using surds. [3]

4 The derivative of a function is given by $\dfrac{dy}{dx} = \dfrac{1}{2}x^2 - \dfrac{3}{\sqrt{x}}$

(i) Find an expression for y if the graph of y against x is to pass through the point $\left(1, \dfrac{1}{6}\right)$. [4]

(ii) Evaluate $\displaystyle\int_0^1 y\,dx$. [4]

5 (i) Rewrite the following expression in the form $f(x) = 0$, where f(x) is of the form $f(x) = ax^3 + bx^2 + cx + d$.

$$(x-1)(x^2 + x + 1) = 2x^2 - 17$$ [2]

(ii) Show that $(x + 2)$ is a factor of f(x). [2]

(iii) Using your answer to part (ii), factorise f(x) as the product of a linear factor and a quadratic factor. [3]

(iv) By completing the square, or otherwise, show that f(x) = 0 has no other real roots. [2]

6 (i) An arithmetic series has first term a and common difference d (where $d > 0$).

    (a) Write down expressions for u_n, u_{n+1} and u_{n+2}, the nth, $(n+1)^{th}$ and $(n+2)^{th}$ terms in the series respectively.   [2]

    (b) By making the substitution $x = a + nd$, write these expressions in terms of x and d only.   [4]

    (c) If the sum of u_n, u_{n+1} and u_{n+2} is 36, and their product is 960, find the values of x and d.   [4]

    (d) If u_n, u_{n+1} and u_{n+2} above are the first three terms of the series, find the value of u_1, and hence

        write down an expression for u_n in terms of n.   [3]

  (ii) Find S_{10}, the sum of the first ten terms of the series.   [3]

  (iii) By considering the formula for S_n and the formula for the sum $\sigma_n = 1 + 2 + 3 + ... + n$, find an expression

     for the difference $S_n - \sigma_n$, giving your answer in as simple a form as possible.   [4]

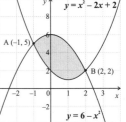

7 This diagram shows the graphs of $y = 6 - x^2$ and $y = x^2 - 2x + 2$.

  (i) Show that the graphs intersect at the points A $(-1, 5)$ and B $(2, 2)$.   [2]

  (ii) Use the trapezium rule with 3 intervals to find approximate values for:

    (a) $\int_{-1}^{2}(6 - x^2)\,dx$ **(b)** $\int_{-1}^{2}(x^2 - 2x + 2)\,dx$

  Hence find an approximate area for the shaded region.   [4]

  (iii) Show that the exact area of the shaded region is given by $\int_{-1}^{2}(-2x^2 + 2x + 4)\,dx$.   [2]

  (iv) Hence, or otherwise, show that the area of the shaded region is 9.   [4]

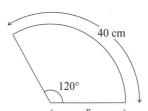

8 The diagram below shows a sector of a circle of radius r cm and angle $120°$.

  The length of the arc of the sector is 40 cm.

  (i) Write $120°$ in radians.   [1]

  (ii) Show that $r \approx 19.1$ cm.   [2]

  (iii) Find the area of the sector to the nearest square centimetre.   [3]

Paper 1 Q1 — Trigonometry

1 (i) By sketching the graph of $y = \tan 2t$ for a suitable range of t, determine the number of solutions to the equation $\tan 2t = k$ in the range $0° \le t < 360°$, where k is any number. [3]

   (ii) Solve the equation $\sin 2t = \sqrt{2} \cos 2t$, giving all the solutions in the range $0° \le t < 360°$. [3]

(i) | A *Squashed up* tan graph

' Sketch the graph of $y = \tan 2t$'

Hmm, that looks suspiciously like $y = \tan x$ to me. Just write t instead of x, and draw the graph <u>twice as squashed</u>.

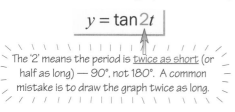

The '2' means the period is <u>twice as short</u> (or half as long) — 90°, not 180°. A common mistake is to draw the graph twice as long.

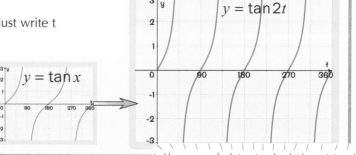

Use your calculator to check the points when the graph should be zero and infinity. If you get an answer you don't expect — stop and think.

It says sketch the graph for a <u>suitable</u> range of t — so sketch the range $0° \le t < 360°$, since that's the range you have to find solutions in.

Think of '*y=k*' — a horizontal line

Now all this is basically asking is, 'how many times does the graph cross the line $y = k$?'.

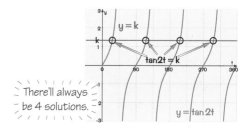

There'll always be 4 solutions.

Now, $y = k$ is just a horizontal line, and it doesn't make any difference exactly where — you can see from the graph that $y = \tan 2t$ will always cross it 4 times in the range $0° \le t < 360°$.

(ii) | It's the *Same Equation*, in disguise

' Solve the equation $\sin 2t = \sqrt{2} \cos 2t$.'

It looks a bit tricky at first, until you realise that if you divide by cos 2t, you get $\tan 2t = \sqrt{2}$ (as $\tan = \frac{\sin}{\cos}$).

The first part of the question was to prepare you to answer this bit.

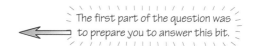

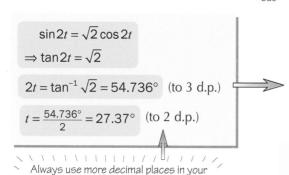

$$\sin 2t = \sqrt{2} \cos 2t$$
$$\Rightarrow \tan 2t = \sqrt{2}$$
$$2t = \tan^{-1}\sqrt{2} = 54.736° \quad \text{(to 3 d.p.)}$$
$$t = \frac{54.736°}{2} = 27.37° \quad \text{(to 2 d.p.)}$$

Always use more decimal places in your workings than you want for your answer — that way you won't make a rounding error.

Whatever you do — <u>don't</u> stop there. That's only one solution, but you know from the first part that there's got to be <u>four</u>. It's not as hard as it sounds, though. The graph <u>repeats</u> itself every 90°, so all you've got to do is add on 90° three times to get the other answers:

So the four solutions to the equation are...

27.37°, 117.37°, 207.37° and 297.37°.

Trig or happy? Trig or treat? Trig or finger? It's just trig-tastic...

There are two important things to be learnt here: Firstly, make sure you know all those standard graphs — then the first part of the question really should be easy. And secondly, if you're stuck on the last part of the question, always look at the earlier bits for hints — it's a pretty safe bet there's going to be some kind of connection that'll help.

Paper 1 Q2 — Logs

2 **(i)** Write down the value of $\log_3 3$ [1]

(ii) Given that $\log_a \chi = \log_a 4 + 3\log_a 2$ show that $\chi = 32$ [2]

(i) $\textbf{\textit{Log}}_3\textbf{3}$ — Some Marks are a Giveaway...

'Write down the value of $\log_3 3$'

This isn't a trick question — they're just checking you know what log means.
From page 16 you should (hopefully) remember that:

> $\log_a b = c$ **means the same as** $a^c = b$
> **That means that** $\log_a a = 1$ **and** $\log_a 1 = 0$

From that bit, it's pretty easy to work out that $\log_3 3 = 1$.

(In other words, $3^1 = 3$, which you should also know from the laws of indices that you did in Core 1.)

(ii) For **Log Equations** you need to **Learn** the **Log Laws**

You'll get the first mark for showing you can use one of the <u>laws of logarithms</u> and the other for successfully getting $\chi = 32$.

OK, let's get stuck in...

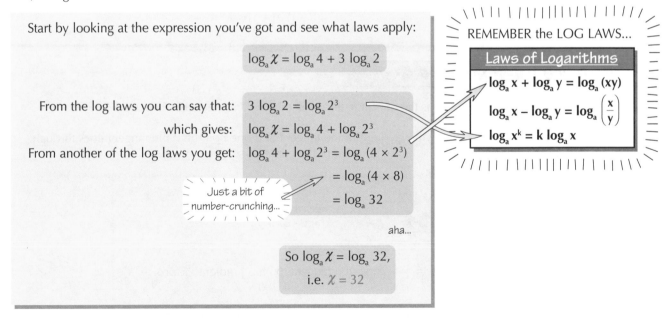

Start by looking at the expression you've got and see what laws apply:

$$\log_a \chi = \log_a 4 + 3\log_a 2$$

REMEMBER the LOG LAWS...

Laws of Logarithms

$\log_a x + \log_a y = \log_a (xy)$

$\log_a x - \log_a y = \log_a \left(\dfrac{x}{y}\right)$

$\log_a x^k = k \log_a x$

From the log laws you can say that: $\quad 3\log_a 2 = \log_a 2^3$

which gives: $\quad \log_a \chi = \log_a 4 + \log_a 2^3$

From another of the log laws you get: $\quad \log_a 4 + \log_a 2^3 = \log_a (4 \times 2^3)$

$$= \log_a (4 \times 8)$$

Just a bit of number-crunching...

$$= \log_a 32$$

aha...

So $\log_a \chi = \log_a 32$,

i.e. $\chi = 32$

AS Maths — (nearly) as easy as falling off a log...

OK, logs aren't the easiest thing in the world, but this is a straightforward question so quit complaining. The best way to prepare for an exam question on logs is to *LEARN THE LOG LAWS*. Whether or not you can apply those laws is kind of irrelevant if you don't know them in the first place. So I repeat: *LEARN THE LOG LAWS*... and *then* practise using them.

Paper 1 Q3 – Integration and Tangents

3 **(i)** Sketch the curve $y = \frac{1}{x^2}$ for $x > 0$. [1]

(ii) Show that $\int_1^\infty \frac{1}{x^2}\, dx = 1$. [2]

(iii) Find the equation of f(x), where f(x) is the tangent to the graph of $y = \frac{1}{x^2}$ at the point where $x = 1$. [2]

(iv) Find $k < 1$ such that $\int_0^k f(x)\,dx = 1$. Give your answer using surds. [3]

(i) It's only a **Sketch** – but get it right

'Sketch the curve $y = \frac{1}{x^2}$ for $x > 0$.'

You need to know what this sort of graph looks like — so this should be <u>easy</u> marks.

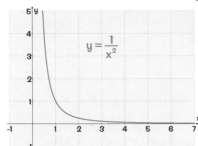

But <u>if</u> you can't remember, you can work it out easily enough:

You need to sketch y for x > 0. So just look at what happens to y:
a) as x gets <u>close to zero</u> and b) as x <u>gets very big</u>.

a) As x gets very large (i.e. tends towards infinity), 1 / x² gets very small.

b) As x tends towards zero, 1/x² tends towards infinity.

(You should use this to check your graph anyway.)

(ii) An integral to **Infinity** – but at least they tell you the answer

'Show that $\int_1^\infty \frac{1}{x^2}\, dx = 1$.'

The integration isn't too bad but take care with the limits, and don't 'lose' any <u>minus signs</u>.

Integrating between 1 and infinity gives...

$$\int_1^\infty \frac{1}{x^2}\, dx = \int_1^\infty x^{-2}\, dx$$

Increase the power by 1 (to make −1) and then divide by −1.

$$= \left[\frac{x^{-1}}{-1}\right]_1^\infty = \left[-\frac{1}{x}\right]_1^\infty$$

$$= (-0) - \left(-\frac{1}{1}\right) = 1$$

Since $\frac{1}{\infty} = 0$.

(iii) Now find a **Tangent** to the curve

'Find the equation of f(x), where f(x) is the tangent to the graph of $y = \frac{1}{x^2}$ at the point where $x = 1$.'

To find a tangent, you just need to know the <u>gradient</u> of the tangent and one <u>point</u> that the tangent goes through. But the gradient of the tangent is the same as the gradient of the curve — so <u>differentiate</u>.

$$y = \frac{1}{x^2} = x^{-2}$$

$$\Rightarrow \frac{dy}{dx} = -2x^{-3} = -\frac{2}{x^3}$$

This is the gradient of the curve y.

The gradient of the curve at x = 1 is $-\frac{2}{1^3} = -2$, so the tangent f(x) has gradient -2 too.

Since f(x) is a straight line, write its equation as f(x) = mx + c, where <u>m</u> is the gradient.

$$f(x) = -2x + c$$

Now you just need to find c.

Paper 1 Q3 — Integration and Tangents

To find c, you need to use the fact that the tangent <u>touches</u> the curve at the point (1, 1).

The lines meet at the point (1, 1), and so

$$f(x) = -2x + c$$
$$\Rightarrow 1 = (-2 \times 1) + c = -2 + c$$

Since f(1) = 1.

$$\Rightarrow c = 3$$

And this means the equation of f(x) is...

$$f(x) = -2x + 3$$

i.e. $\quad f(x) = 3 - 2x$

This means the same but looks a bit neater.

(iv) Another **Integration** — but this time you have to find the **Upper Limit**

'Find $k < 1$ such that $\int_0^k f(x)\,dx = 1$. Give your answer using surds.'

Now you need to find a value less than 1 for k. Just do the integration <u>normally</u> but write k instead of a number...

$$\int_0^k f(x)\,dx = \int_0^k (3 - 2x)\,dx$$
$$= \left[3x - x^2 \right]_0^k$$
$$= (3k - k^2) - 0$$
$$= 3k - k^2$$

Don't do anything differently just because you have k instead of a number.

This integral has to be equal to 1, so you need to solve

$$3k - k^2 = 1$$
$$\Rightarrow k^2 - 3k + 1 = 0$$

Since the question asks you to find k such that $\int_0^k f(x)\,dx = 1$.

This is a <u>quadratic</u>, and the question mentions <u>surds</u> — so it doesn't look as though it's going to factorise.

Using the quadratic formula...

$$k = \frac{3 \pm \sqrt{(-3)^2 - 4 \times 1 \times 1}}{2 \times 1}$$
$$= \frac{3 \pm \sqrt{5}}{2}$$

There are two possible values for k here — you have to decide which one you need.

The question says k has to be less than 1 — so use a calculator to work out which of these possible values you need.

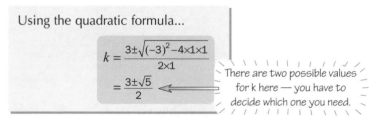

$$\frac{3 + \sqrt{5}}{2} = 2.618 \qquad \frac{3 - \sqrt{5}}{2} = 0.382$$

So this is the one you need.

The question asks you to give your final answer in <u>surds</u>, though.

And so the required value of k is

$$k = \frac{3 - \sqrt{5}}{2}$$

---

f(x)? Can't they think of a better name? Like Trevor. Yes — Trevor The Tangent

Phew. I mean, really... phew. What a stinker. Let's break it down. <u>Part i)</u> — you really should know what graphs like y = kxⁿ look like — but you can work it out anyway if you just choose a few values for x, work out the value of y there, and then plot the points. <u>Part ii)</u> It's just a limit integration. Don't be put off by the ∞ — it only comes into play when you're substituting in the limits at the end (where you have to use the fact that 1/∞ is 0). <u>Part iii)</u> is okay really. Nuff said. <u>Part iv)</u> — well it's long. And you get two answers at the end when you might only expect one. When this happens, have another look at the question and see if you can get rid of one somehow. Here, they only want a value of k that's less than 1 — so you can get rid of the one that's bigger than 1. Obvious, eh? — but easily forgotten in the exam.

Paper 1 Q4 — Calculus

4   The derivative of a function is given by

$$\frac{dy}{dx} = \frac{1}{2}x^2 - \frac{3}{\sqrt{x}}$$

   (i)   Find an expression for y if the graph of y against x is to pass through the point $\left(1, \frac{1}{6}\right)$.   [4]

   (ii)   Evaluate $\int_0^1 y\,dx$.   [4]

(i)   *You just Integrate it...*

'Find an expression for *y* if the graph of *y* against *x* is to pass through the point $\left(1, \frac{1}{6}\right)$.'

To get an expression for y from an expression for $\frac{dy}{dx}$, you just <u>integrate</u>.

(Integration is the opposite of differentiation, remember.)

Before you can integrate it, you have to rewrite $\frac{dy}{dx}$ as <u>powers of x</u>...

$$\frac{dy}{dx} = \frac{1}{2}x^2 - \frac{3}{\sqrt{x}}$$

$$= \frac{1}{2}x^2 - 3x^{-\frac{1}{2}}$$

> Rewrite that square root as a power of x.

Now write both sides as integrals...

> Just put an integral sign and 'dx' around both sides for now.

$$\int \frac{dy}{dx}\,dx = \int\left(\frac{1}{2}x^2 - 3x^{-\frac{1}{2}}\right)dx$$

Integrate the left-hand side and you get y.
And you can rewrite the right-hand side to break it into smaller bits...

$$y = \frac{1}{2}\int x^2\,dx - 3\int x^{-\frac{1}{2}}\,dx$$

> Integrating $\frac{dy}{dx}$ gives y.

> You only need to look at the x bits, so you can put the numbers outside the integration signs.

Now just integrate both terms on the right-hand side.

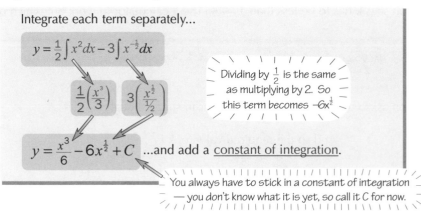

Integrate each term separately...

$$y = \frac{1}{2}\int x^2\,dx - 3\int x^{-\frac{1}{2}}\,dx$$

The integration formula:

$$\int x^n\,dx = \frac{x^{n+1}}{n+1} + C$$

$$\frac{1}{2}\left(\frac{x^3}{3}\right) \qquad 3\left(\frac{x^{\frac{1}{2}}}{\frac{1}{2}}\right)$$

> Dividing by $\frac{1}{2}$ is the same as multiplying by 2. So this term becomes $-6x^{\frac{1}{2}}$

$$y = \frac{x^3}{6} - 6x^{\frac{1}{2}} + C \quad \text{...and add a } \underline{\text{constant of integration}}.$$

> You always have to stick in a constant of integration — you don't know what it is yet, so call it C for now.

You might wonder why there's only one constant. Since you've had to do three separate mini-integrations, shouldn't there be three constants like this?

$$y + C_1 = \frac{x^3}{6} + C_2 - 6x^{\frac{1}{2}} + C_3$$

Well yes, but rather than have three separate ones, you can just make them into one.

Let $C = -C_1 + C_2 + C_3 \Rightarrow y = \frac{x^3}{6} - 6x^{\frac{1}{2}} + C$

Paper 1 Q4 — Calculus

...and then stick in the Values it gives for x and y

Now you've got to find C. The question says it's got to 'pass through the point $\left(1, \frac{1}{6}\right)$.'

In other words: when $x = 1$, $y = \frac{1}{6}$. Sticking this in will give you the value of C:

Substitute $x = 1$ and $y = \frac{1}{6}$ in the expression for y...

$$\frac{1}{6} = \frac{1^3}{6} - \left(6 \times 1^{\frac{1}{2}}\right) + C$$

$$= \frac{1}{6} - 6 + C$$

$$\Rightarrow C = 6$$

And so the complete expression for y is...

$$y = \frac{x^3}{6} - 6x^{\frac{1}{2}} + 6$$

You should check your answer by:

(i) putting in $x = 1$ (and making sure you get $\frac{1}{6}$)

and   (ii) differentiating it (and making sure you get the derivative in the question).

(ii) A simple Limit Integral — but don't fall into the Trap

'Evaluate $\displaystyle\int_0^1 y\,dx$.'

This part is pretty standard stuff — but there's a really obvious trap at the start. As long as you avoid that, you can't go far wrong.

The Trap:

$$\int_0^1 y\,dx = \left[\frac{y^2}{2}\right]_0^1 = \frac{1}{2} - 0 = \frac{1}{2}$$

This is rubbish! — because this is integrating with respect to y, not x.

The Right Way:

$$\int_0^1 y\,dx.$$

The 'dx' means you're integrating with respect to x. So you need to write y in terms of x before you integrate. (i.e. stick in the answer to part (i).)

$$\int_0^1 y\,dx = \int_0^1 \left(\frac{x^3}{6} - 6x^{\frac{1}{2}} + 6\right) dx$$

You could break this up into individual chunks like before — but you don't have to. Do whatever's easier.

It's a limit integral, so integrate the bracket — and stick it in a big square bracket with limits.

$$\int_0^1 y\,dx = \int_0^1 \left(\frac{x^3}{6} - 6x^{\frac{1}{2}} + 6\right) dx = \left[\frac{x^4}{6 \times 4} - \frac{6x^{\frac{3}{2}}}{\frac{3}{2}} + \frac{6x^1}{1}\right]_0^1$$

$$= \left[\frac{x^4}{24} - 4x^{\frac{3}{2}} + 6x\right]_0^1$$

$\frac{6}{\frac{3}{2}} = 6 \times \frac{2}{3} = \frac{12}{3} = 4$

Now evaluate the square bracket — use the top limit first, then subtract what you get when you use the bottom limit.

$$\int_0^1 y\,dx = \left(\frac{1^4}{24} - \left(4 \times 1^{\frac{3}{2}}\right) + (6 \times 1)\right) - \left(\frac{0^4}{24} - \left(4 \times 0^{\frac{3}{2}}\right) + (6 \times 0)\right)$$

$$= \frac{1}{24} - 4 + 6$$

$$= \frac{49}{24}$$

When you put $x = 0$, all these parts are equal to zero.

$\frac{1}{24} - 4 + 6 = \frac{1}{24} + 2 = \frac{48 + 1}{24} = \frac{49}{24}$

Integration — Int it great? ...no? Oh... didn't think so...

This question is a gift — it's all real standard stuff. So if you're struggling with it, bury your head in those maths books until it begins to make sense. And another thing — always make sure you use all the info the question gives you, e.g. if it says the graph passes through the point (joe, bloggs), it means "at some point in the question, you need to plug in the values x=joe when y=bloggs". And watch for that trap at the end — the 'dx' in an integral means you have to integrate x's.

Paper 1 Q5 — Algebra

5 **(i)** Rewrite the following expression in the form $f(x) = 0$, where $f(x)$ is of the form $f(x) = ax^3 + bx^2 + cx + d$.

$$(x-1)(x^2+x+1) = 2x^2 - 17$$

[2]

(ii) Show that $(x+2)$ is a factor of $f(x)$. [2]

(iii) Using your answer to part (ii), factorise $f(x)$ as the product of a linear factor and a quadratic factor. [3]

(iv) By completing the square, or otherwise, show that $f(x) = 0$ has no other real roots. [2]

(i) Multiply out the Brackets and get everything on one side

'Rewrite the following expression in the form $f(x) = 0$ ...'

Looks confusing, but all it's asking you to do is multiply out the brackets and then rearrange it to get <u>zero</u> on one side.

Start by multiplying out the tricky bit:

$$(x-1)(x^2+x+1) = x(x^2+x+1) - 1(x^2+x+1)$$
$$= x^3 + x^2 + x - x^2 - x - 1$$
$$= x^3 - 1$$

Write out the thing you're starting from:

$$(x-1)(x^2+x+1) = 2x^2 - 17$$

You've just worked out this bit:

$$\Rightarrow x^3 - 1 = 2x^2 - 17$$
$$\Rightarrow x^3 - 2x^2 + 16 = 0$$

... and take everything over to one side.

This is in the form f(x) = 0, if f(x) is:

$$f(x) = x^3 - 2x^2 + 16$$

a = 1   b = –2
c = 0   d = 16

... and f(x) is in the form ax³ + bx² + cx + d...

... so your answer is: $x^3 - 2x^2 + 16 = 0$

(ii) Show that something's a Factor — you need the Factor Theorem

'Show that (x + 2) is a factor of *f(x)*.'

Whenever you see the word 'factor' in a question — think '<u>Factor Theorem</u>'.
There's ALWAYS a question on it. Which is good — cos it's easy.

See page 2 for more about the Fabulous Factor Theorem.

To show whether (x + 2) is a factor of f(x), find f(–2)...

$$f(x) = x^3 - 2x^2 + 16$$
$$\Rightarrow f(-2) = (-2)^3 - 2\times(-2)^2 + 16$$
$$= -8 - 8 + 16$$
$$= 0$$

Since f(–2) = 0, by the Factor Theorem, (x + 2) must be a factor of f(x).

The Factor Theorem (in case you've forgotten it...)

The Factor Theorem says that (x – a) is a factor of a polynomial f(x) if and only if f(a) = 0.

So if you want to show that (x+2) is a factor of f(x), just show that f(–2) = 0.

But don't get the plus and minus signs confused...

To prove that (x+a) is a factor, show f(–a) = 0.   To prove that (x–a) is a factor, show f(a) = 0.

Paper 1 Q5 — Algebra

(iii) Now you need to Factorise a Cubic

'Using your answer to part (ii), factorise *f(x)* as the product of a linear factor and a quadratic factor.'

From part (ii), you know that (x + 2) is a factor of f(x). So...

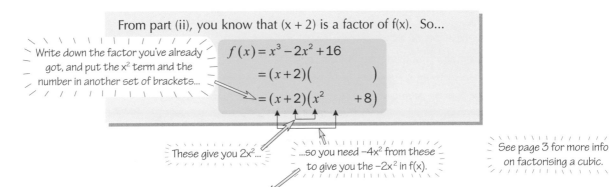

Write down the factor you've already got, and put the x² term and the number in another set of brackets...

$$f(x) = x^3 - 2x^2 + 16$$
$$= (x+2)(\qquad)$$
$$= (x+2)(x^2 \qquad +8)$$

These give you 2x²...

...so you need –4x² from these to give you the –2x² in f(x).

See page 3 for more info on factorising a cubic.

So put the –4x you need in the middle of the quadratic term and you get: $f(x) = (x+2)(x^2 - 4x + 8)$

(iv) And for my next trick, I shall Complete the Square...

'By completing the square, or otherwise, show that f(*x*) = 0 has no other roots, and sketch the graph of f(*x*).'

Now you've factorised f(x), the next bit's not too bad.

$$f(x) = (x+2)(x^2 - 4x + 8)$$
so $f(x) = 0$ when $(x+2) = 0$ or $(x^2 - 4x + 8) = 0$.

You've already shown that f(x) = 0 when x + 2 = 0.
So, to show that f(x) = 0 doesn't have any <u>other</u> roots,
you need to show that x² – 4x + 8 is <u>never zero</u>.

The question gives you the hint that completing the square will be useful — so try that...

Completing the square with x² – 4x + 8: $x^2 - 4x + 8 = (x-2)^2 + something$
$$= (x-2)^2 + 4$$

(x – 2)² = x² – 4x + 4, so you need an extra four.

Since (x – 2)² can never be less than zero, the smallest value this can take is 4, and so it can definitely never be zero. So that means that <u>f(x)=0 has no other solutions</u>.

Now you've finished the question. You star!

Well actually, I did the question and you just read it.
So you're only a little star.

That's you that is.

The question's over — Am I not merciful... AM I NOT MERCIFUL...?

The main thing to take from this page is that the Factor Theorem will definitely be in your exam. I kid you not — it'll be there. And I reckon anyone who knew that would definitely make sure they knew what the Factor Theorem was all about before the exam — especially since it's not even that hard. Think about it — guaranteed marks on a plate. Can't be bad.

Paper 1 Q6 — Arithmetic Series

6 (i) An arithmetic series has first term a and common difference d (where $d > 0$).

    (a) Write down expressions for u_n, u_{n+1} and u_{n+2}, the nth, $(n+1)^{th}$ and $(n+2)^{th}$ terms in the series respectively.   **[2]**

    (b) By making the substitution $x = a + nd$, write these expressions in terms of x and d only.   **[4]**

    (c) If the sum of u_n, u_{n+1} and u_{n+2} is 36, and their product is 960, find the values of x and d.   **[4]**

    (d) If u_n, u_{n+1} and u_{n+2} above are the first three terms of the series, find the value of u_1, and hence write down an expression for u_n in terms of n.   **[3]**

  (ii) Find S_{10}, the sum of the first ten terms of the series.   **[3]**

  (iii) By considering the formula for S_n and the formula for the sum $\sigma_n = 1 + 2 + 3 + \ldots + n$, find an expression for the difference $S_n - \sigma_n$, giving your answer in as simple a form as possible.   **[4]**

(i)(a)   The nth Term of an Arithmetic Series — piece of cake

'Write down expressions for u_n, u_{n+1} and u_{n+2}...'

The question uses the words '<u>write down</u>' (not 'work out' or 'find', or anything like that) — so you should just be able to quote the answer without thinking about it.

For an arithmetic series, the nth term is just: $u_n = a + (n-1)d$, so...

$$u_n = a + (n-1)d$$
$$u_{n+1} = a + nd$$
$$u_{n+2} = a + (n+1)d$$

⟵ Use the same formula each time, but substitute (n+1) and (n+2) for n.
E.g. u_{n+1} = a + [(n + 1) − 1]d = a + nd, etc.

(i)(b)   Substitute — and then Rewrite

'By making the substitution $x = a + nd$, write these expressions in terms of x and d only.'

So you've got to rewrite those same expressions, but with only x and d on the right-hand side. But at least it tells you how to do it — by writing x instead of 'a + nd'.

$$u_n = a + (n-1)d = a + nd - d = x - d$$
$$u_{n+1} = a + nd = x$$
$$u_{n+2} = a + (n+1)d = a + nd + d = x + d$$

Work out the brackets in the answers to part (i), and then write x wherever you see 'a+nd'.

(i)(c)   Fiddle About a bit to find x and d

'If the sum of u_n, u_{n+1} and u_{n+2} is 36, and their product is 960, find the values of x and d.'

This looks hard — but there are some big clues in the question. It tells you what the <u>sum</u> and <u>product</u> of the expressions in part (b) equal — so start by working those out...

The sum is:
$$u_n + u_{n+1} + u_{n+2} = (x - d) + x + (x + d)$$
$$= 3x$$

And this equals 36, so...
$$3x = 36$$
$$\Rightarrow x = 12$$

> The <u>sum</u> of a load of numbers is what you get when you <u>add</u> them all together.
>
> The <u>product</u> of a load of numbers is what you get when you <u>multiply</u> them all together.

The product is:
$$u_n \times u_{n+1} \times u_{n+2} = (x - d)x(x + d)$$
$$= x(x^2 - d^2)$$

Using the difference of two squares:
$(x + d)(x - d) = x^2 - d^2$.

This equals 960. But you've just worked out that x = 12 — so put this value in as well...

$$x(x^2 - d^2) = 960$$
$$\Rightarrow 12(144 - d^2) = 960$$

This only has one letter left to find, d.

And now you can find the value of d...
$$\Rightarrow 144 - d^2 = 80 \quad \left(\tfrac{960}{12} = 80\right)$$
$$\Rightarrow d^2 = 144 - 80 = 64$$
$$\Rightarrow d = 8$$

Paper 1 Q6 — Arithmetic Series

(i)(d) | *Now find the **First Term** using your answers from before...*

'...find the value of u_1, and hence write down an expression for u_n in terms of n.'

If u_n, u_{n+1} and u_{n+2} are the first three terms of the series, then $\quad u_1 = u_n = x - d = 12 - 8 = 4$

Using your answers from parts (b) and (c).

...which means the nth term of the series is: $\quad u_n = a + (n-1)d = 4 + 8(n-1)$

$$= 4 + 8n - 8 = 8n - 4$$

You've just worked out that the first term of the series u_1 (= a) is 4.

(ii) | ***Sum** an arithmetic series*

'Find S_{10}, the sum of the first ten terms of the series.'

This is an absolute doddle — as long as you know the formula for the sum of the first n terms of an arithmetic series...

The formula for the sum of the first n terms of an arithmetic series is:

$$S_n = \frac{n}{2}[2a + (n-1)d]$$

This is the general formula for the sum of the first n terms...

Or you can use the other formula for the sum of the first n terms of an arithmetic series:
$$S_n = \frac{n}{2}(a+l).$$

And so if n = 10: $\quad S_{10} = 5[2a + 9d]$

...so if you only want the sum of the first ten terms, use this one.

Putting in the values of a (= 4) and d (= 8), you get...

$$S_{10} = 5[(2 \times 4) + (9 \times 8)]$$
$$= 5 \times 80 = 400$$

(iii) | *What do the examiners want now — Blood...*

'...find an expression for the difference $S_n - \sigma_n$...'

Right then — now it's serious. This bit looks nasty — but just do it one bit at a time.

You've already got the formula for S_n. It is:

$$S_n = \frac{n}{2}[2a + (n-1)d]$$

And since you know a = 4 and d = 8, this becomes:

$$S_n = \frac{n}{2}[8 + 8(n-1)]$$
$$= \frac{n}{2}[8 + 8n - 8]$$
$$= \frac{n}{2}(8n) = 4n^2$$

Now $\sigma_n = 1 + 2 + 3 + ... + n$, and you should know that this sum is given by:

$$\sigma_n = 1 + 2 + ... + n = \sum_{i=1}^{n} i = \frac{n}{2}(n+1)$$

You'll need to remember this formula.

And all the question's actually asking you to do is work out $S_n - \sigma_n$. This is just:

$$S_n - \sigma_n = 4n^2 - \frac{n}{2}(n+1)$$
$$= 4n^2 - \frac{n^2}{2} - \frac{n}{2}$$
$$= \frac{7}{2}n^2 - \frac{n}{2}$$
$$= \frac{n}{2}(7n - 1)$$

Taking a factor of $\frac{n}{2}$ outside the brackets.

Check your answer: choose n = 3.
$S_3 = 4 + 12 + 20 = 36$.
$\sigma_3 = 1 + 2 + 3 = 6$.
According to your formula the difference between them should be: $\frac{3}{2}((7 \times 3) - 1) = 30$. And since $36 - 6 = 30$, this works.

When the question says jump — you ask, 'How high...'

A lot of questions look mean, but when you get past the 'maths-speak' they're not really so bad. When they give 'advice' on tackling a problem, it's a good idea to take it — do as you're told, basically. Also, with this question (like a load of others), you can check your answer by choosing a (small) value for n and seeing if your formula works. Then if it does work, you can do the next question with a warm happy feeling inside. Wonderful...

Paper 1 Q7 — Areas Between Curves

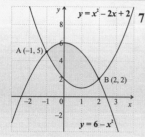

7 This diagram shows the graphs of $y = 6 - x^2$ and $y = x^2 - 2x + 2$.

(i) Show that the graphs intersect at the points A $(-1, 5)$ and B $(2, 2)$. **[2]**

(ii) Use the trapezium rule with 3 intervals to find approximate values for:

(a) $\int_{-1}^{2} (6 - x^2)\, dx$ **(b)** $\int_{-1}^{2} (x^2 - 2x + 2)\, dx$

Hence find an approximate area for the shaded region. **[4]**

(iii) Show that the exact area of the shaded region is given by $\int_{-1}^{2} (-2x^2 + 2x + 4)\, dx$. **[2]**

(iv) Hence, or otherwise, show that the area of the shaded region is 9. **[4]**

(i)   Substitute the x-values into the Equations

'Show that the graphs intersect at the points A$(-1, 5)$ and B$(2, 2)$.'

The graphs will intersect at A$(-1, 5)$ and B$(2, 2)$ if both graphs pass through those points.

To show that, you need to substitute the *x*-coordinates into the equations and show that they give you the correct *y*-coordinates.

Starting with:	$y = 6 - x^2$		$y = 6 - x^2$
When $x = -1$:	$y = 6 - (-1)^2$	and when $x = 2$:	$y = 6 - 2^2$
	$y = 6 - 1 = 5$		$y = 6 - 4 = 2$

So the graph of $y = 6 - x^2$ passes through A$(-1, 5)$ and B$(2, 2)$.

Now for the other graph:

	$y = x^2 - 2x + 2$		$y = x^2 - 2x + 2$
When $x = -1$,	$y = (-1)^2 - 2(-1) + 2$	and when $x = 2$,	$y = 2^2 - 2(2) + 2$
	$y = 1 + 2 + 2 = 5$		$y = 4 - 4 + 2 = 2$

So this graph also passes through A$(-1, 5)$ and B$(2, 2)$.

Both graphs pass through A$(-1, 5)$ and B$(2, 2)$ — and so they intersect at those points.

(ii)   Look up the Trapezium Rule and work out the Values you need

'Use the trapezium rule with 3 intervals to find approximate values for: **(a)** $\int_{-1}^{2} (6 - x^2)\, dx$ **(b)** $\int_{-1}^{2} (x^2 - 2x + 2)\, dx$
Hence find an approximate area for the shaded region.'

Here's your strategy:

> Job 1 — Find the area under each of the graphs.
> Job 2 — Subtract one from the other to get the shaded area.

It's easier to understand if you look at the graphs.

The area under $y = 6 - x^2$...   ...minus the area under $y = x^2 - 2x + 2$...   ...equals the shaded region:

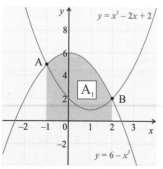
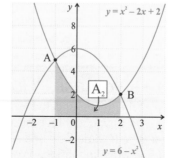
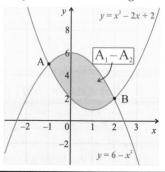

Paper 1 Q7 — Areas Between Curves

Job 1) You have to use the trapezium rule twice. Parts (a) and (b) are basically the same but with two different equations, so everything will be the same except the y-values.

(a) $\int_{-1}^{2}(6-x^2)\,dx$

Start by looking up the formula for the trapezium rule in the formula booklet, then write it down:

$$\int_{a}^{b} y\,dx \approx \frac{h}{2}\left[y_0 + 2(y_1 + y_2 + \ldots + y_{n-1}) + y_n\right]$$

n is the number of intervals
h is the width of each strip

The question tells you to use 3 intervals between $x = -1$ and $x = 2$, so that means $n = 3$, and $a = -1$ and $b = 2$.

The width of each strip is $h = \dfrac{(2--1)}{3} = 1$.

Now work out the y values:

x	$y = 6 - x^2$
$x_0 = -1$	$y_0 = 6 - (-1)^2 = 5$
$x_1 = 0$	$y_1 = 6 - 0^2 = 6$
$x_2 = 1$	$y_2 = 6 - 1^2 = 5$
$x_3 = 2$	$y_3 = 6 - 2^2 = 2$

Finally, put all these values into the formula:

$$A_1 = \int_{-1}^{2}(6-x^2)\,dx$$
$$\approx \frac{1}{2}\left[5 + 2(6+5) + 2\right]$$
$$= \frac{1}{2}(5 + 22 + 2)$$
$$= \frac{29}{2} = 14.5$$

(b) $\int_{-1}^{2}(x^2 - 2x + 2)\,dx$

Now just work out some new y values:

x	$y = x^2 - 2x + 2$
$x_0 = -1$	$y_0 = (-1)^2 - 2(-1) + 2 = 5$
$x_1 = 0$	$y_1 = 0^2 - 2(0) + 2 = 2$
$x_2 = 1$	$y_2 = 1^2 - 2(1) + 2 = 1$
$x_3 = 2$	$y_3 = 2^2 - 2(2) + 2 = 2$

...and put these values into the formula:

$$A_2 = \int_{-1}^{2}(x^2 - 2x + 2)\,dx$$
$$\approx \frac{1}{2}\left[5 + 2(2+1) + 2\right]$$
$$= \frac{13}{2} = 6.5$$

Job 2) You can now find the shaded area by subtracting: **Shaded area = $A_1 - A_2 \approx 14.5 - 6.5 = 8$**

(iii) *Subtract one expression from the other for the area between the two graphs*

'Show that the exact area of the shaded region is given by $\int_{-1}^{2}(-2x^2 + 2x + 4)\,dx$.'

1) You're not asked for a numerical value — just to find an expression to work out the area.

2) In part (ii) you found an approximation for the shaded area by **subtracting** — you do the same here but using algebra.

3) Just like part (ii), the shaded area is $A_1 - A_2$, but to work out the exact values you need to **integrate**.

$$A_1 = \int_{-1}^{2}(6-x^2)\,dx \;,\;\; A_2 = \int_{-1}^{2}(x^2 - 2x + 2)\,dx$$
$$A = A_1 - A_2 = \int_{-1}^{2}\left[(6-x^2)-(x^2-2x+2)\right]dx$$
$$= \int_{-1}^{2}(-2x^2 + 2x + 4)\,dx$$

Because the limits are the same, you can subtract inside the integration.

(iv) *Now use what you've just worked out to finish things off*

'Hence, or otherwise, show that the area of the shaded region is 9.'

'Hence' always means, 'use what you've just worked out'. Here you have to integrate the expression from part (iii).

$$\int_{-1}^{2}(-2x^2 + 2x + 4)\,dx = \left[-\frac{2}{3}x^3 + x^2 + 4x\right]_{-1}^{2}$$
$$= \left(-\frac{2}{3}\times 2^3 + 2^2 + 4(2)\right) - \left(-\frac{2}{3}\times(-1)^3 + (-1)^2 + 4(-1)\right)$$
$$= \left(-\frac{16}{3} + 4 + 8\right) - \left(\frac{2}{3} + 1 - 4\right)$$

Take care with all the minus signs.

$$= 6\frac{2}{3} - \left(-2\frac{1}{3}\right) = 9$$

However bad it gets...

Keep reminding yourself — AS Maths looks great on your CV.

Paper 1 Q8 — Sector Areas

8 The diagram below shows a sector of a circle of radius r cm and angle 120°.
The length of the arc of the sector is 40 cm.

(i) Write 120° in radians. [1]

(ii) Show that $r \approx 19.1$ cm. [2]

(iii) Find the area of the sector to the nearest square centimetre. [3]

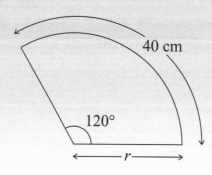

40 cm

120°

r

(i) Use 360° = 2π Radians to Convert from Degrees to Radians

'Write 120° in radians.'

The first thing to notice is that the question says 'Write...'. This means you don't need to do any complicated working out — you can just give your answer in terms of π.

Now lots of people get in a tizz with **conversion factors**, but you will have to do them, so it's a good idea to have a **sure-fire method** up your sleeve. This is the way I do it:

1) You know that $360° = 2\pi$, so the conversion factor is either going to be $\frac{2\pi}{360}$ or $\frac{360}{2\pi}$.

2) You're converting 120° into radians, so you're going to expect a **smaller** number than 120 when you've done the conversion.

3) If you want the conversion factor to give you a smaller number, it must be less than 1 (i.e. the top of the fraction must be smaller than the bottom). Well, $2\pi \approx 2 \times 3 = 6$, which is obviously less than 360, so you need to use the **first** conversion factor $\left(\frac{2\pi}{360}\right)$:

$$120° = 120° \times \frac{2\pi}{360°} \text{ radians}$$

$$= \frac{120°}{360°} \times 2\pi \text{ radians}$$

$$= \frac{1}{3} \times 2\pi \text{ radians}$$

$$= \frac{2\pi}{3} \text{ radians}$$

The formulas you're going to use for parts (ii) and (iii) need the angles to be measured in radians, so the first part of the question sets this up.

Paper 1 Q8 — Sector Areas

(ii) | Remember the formula

'Show that $r \approx 19.1$ cm.'

You know the angle (θ) and the arc length (S), so you can use this formula to find the radius (r):

$$S = r\theta$$

Substituting S = 40 cm and $\theta = \dfrac{2\pi}{3}$ gives: $40 = \dfrac{2\pi}{3} \times r$

Then divide both sides by $\dfrac{2\pi}{3}$: $r = 40 \div \dfrac{2\pi}{3}$

$= 40 \div 2.094$

$= 19.1$ cm (3 s.f.)

Don't throw marks away by forgetting the units.

(iii) | Now use the other Formula to find the Area of the Sector

'Find the area of the sector to the nearest square centimetre.'

You've got the radius from part (ii), so you can stick it in the formula for the area of the sector...

...which, as I'm sure you've remembered, is this: $A = \dfrac{1}{2}r^2\theta$

The more decimal places you keep in your calculations, the more accurate your answer will be.

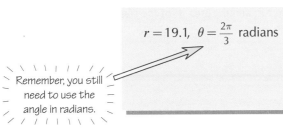

$r = 19.1$, $\theta = \dfrac{2\pi}{3}$ radians

$A = \dfrac{1}{2} \times (19.099)^2 \times \dfrac{2\pi}{3}$

$= \dfrac{1}{2} \times 364.77 \times 2.094$

$= 382$ cm^2 (to the nearest cm^2)

Remember, you still need to use the angle in radians.

If you can't remember which formula's which between '$r\theta$' and '$\dfrac{1}{2}r^2\theta$', think about which one's a **length** and which one's an **area**. The expression '$r\theta$' has just **one length** in it (r), so it must represent the arc **length** (S). The expression '$\dfrac{1}{2}r^2\theta$' has **two lengths** (r^2), so it must be the **area** of a sector.

Another handy tip...

If you're not sure if you've remembered the area formula properly, put in 2π for θ and make sure it gives you πr^2, because $2\pi = 360° = $ a full circle. You can also use this to work out the formula in reverse: $\dfrac{\theta}{2\pi} \times \pi r^2 = \dfrac{1}{2}r^2\theta$.

Alternatively, of course, you can just learn them, which might be easier.

General Certificate of Education
Advanced Subsidiary (AS) and Advanced Level

Core 2 Mathematics — Practice Exam Two

Give non-exact numerical answers correct to 3 significant figures, unless a
different degree of accuracy is specified in the question or is clearly appropriate.

---

1 (i) Rewrite the following equation in the form $f(x) = 0$, where $f(x)$ is of the form $f(x) = ax^2 + bx + c$.

$$(x-1)(x-4) = 2x^2 + 11$$ [2]

(ii) By completing the square, or otherwise, show that $f(x) = 0$ has no real roots. [2]

(iii) Sketch the graph of $f(x)$. Evaluate the area enclosed by the graph of $f(x)$, the line $y = \frac{1}{\sqrt{2}}$,
the line $x = \sqrt{2}$ and the y-axis. [4]

2 (i) Sketch the graph of $y = \cos(x - 60°)$ for x between $0°$ and $360°$. [2]

(ii) Show that the equation

$$2\sin^2(x - 60°) = 1 + \cos(x - 60°)$$ may be written as a quadratic in $\cos(x - 60°)$. [4]

(iii) Hence solve this equation, giving all values of x such that $0° \le x \le 360°$. [4]

3 A new symmetrical mini-stage is to be built according to the design shown below. The design consists of a rectangle of length q metres and width $2r$ metres, two sectors of radius r and angle θ radians (shaded), and an isoceles triangle.

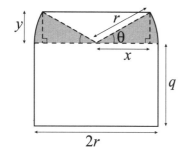

(i) (a) Show that distance x is given by $x = r\cos\theta$. [2]

(b) Find a similar expression for distance y. [2]

(ii) Find in terms of r, q and θ, expressions for the
perimeter P, and the area A, of the stage. [3]

4 (i) Write down the first four terms in the expansion of $(1 + ax)^{10}$, a > 0. [2]

(ii) Find the coefficient of x^2 in the expansion of $(2 + 3x)^5$. [2]

(iii) If the coefficients of x^2 in both expansions are equal, find the value of a. [2]

5 The diagram shows the graph of $y = 2^{x^2}$.

(i) Use the trapezium rule with 4 intervals to find an estimate for the
area of the region bounded by the axes, the curve and the line x = 2. [4]

(ii) State whether the estimate in (i) is an overestimate or
an underestimate, giving a reason for your answer. [2]

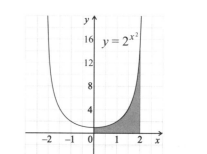

6 **(i)** An arithmetic series has first term a and common difference d.

Prove that the sum of the first n terms, S_n, is given by the formula $S_n = \dfrac{n}{2}[2a + (n-1)d]$. [4]

(ii) Evaluate $\displaystyle\sum_{n=9}^{32} 2n - 5$. [4]

7 A geometric series $u_1 + u_2 + \dots + u_n$ has 3rd term $\dfrac{5}{2}$ and 6th term $\dfrac{5}{16}$.

(i) Find the common ratio and the first term of the series. Hence give the formula for the nth term of the series. [4]

(ii) Find $\displaystyle\sum_{n=1}^{10} u_n$. Give your answer as a fraction in its simplest terms. [3]

(iii) Show that the sum to infinity of the series is 20. [2]

8 **(i)** **(a)** Show that the graph of $f(x) = -x^2(x-2)$ has turning points at the origin and the point $\left(\dfrac{4}{3}, \dfrac{32}{27}\right)$. [3]

(b) Sketch the graph of $f(x)$, marking in any turning points and points where it crosses the axes. [2]

(ii) The function $g(x)$ is defined by $g(x) = 2 - x$. Given that the graphs of $f(x)$ and $g(x)$ meet at $x = 1$, sketch the graph of $g(x)$ on the same set of axes you used in part (i), marking in the coordinates of the two points of intersection for which x is positive. [3]

(iii) Show that the area enclosed by the two graphs between $x = 1$ and $x = 2$ is $\dfrac{5}{12}$. [3]

9 **(i)** Find the missing length a in the triangle. [4]

(ii) Find the angles θ and ϕ. [3]

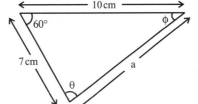

Paper 2 Q1 — Graphs and Integration

1 (i) Rewrite the following equation in the form $f(x) = 0$, where $f(x)$ is of the form $f(x) = ax^2 + bx + c$.

$$(x-1)(x-4) = 2x^2 + 11$$ [2]

(ii) By completing the square, or otherwise, show that $f(x) = 0$ has no real roots. [2]

(iii) Sketch the graph of $f(x)$. Evaluate the area enclosed by the graph of $f(x)$, the line $y = \frac{1}{\sqrt{2}}$,

the line $x = \sqrt{2}$ and the y-axis. [4]

(i) The first part's *Really Simple*

'Rewrite the following equation in the form $f(x) = 0$, where f(x) is of the form $f(x) = ax^2 + bx + c$.'
$$(x-1)(x-4) = 2x^2 + 11$$

The first thing to do is get rid of the brackets. So multiply them out:

$$x^2 - 5x + 4 = 2x^2 + 11$$

And rearrange, putting everything on one side (you want zero on the right-hand side).

$$-x^2 - 5x - 7 = 0$$
$$\Rightarrow x^2 + 5x + 7 = 0$$

And that's part (i) done. (So a=1, b=5, and c=7.)

(ii) *Complete* the Square and *Use* it

'By completing the square, or otherwise, show that $f(x) = 0$ has no roots.'

So f(x) = x²+5x+7 from part (i). The <u>question</u> says to complete the square, so let's not argue.

Write the squared bracket down with d added.

$$\left(x + \tfrac{5}{2}\right)^2 + d \quad \longleftarrow \text{ d is some unknown number.}$$

You need to find a value for d such that $\left(x + \tfrac{5}{2}\right)^2 + d = f(x)$

So put in the old expression for f(x):

$$\left(x + \tfrac{5}{2}\right)^2 + d = x^2 + 5x + 7$$

and solve it to find d...

$$x^2 + 5x + \tfrac{25}{4} + d = x^2 + 5x + 7$$
$$d = 7 - \tfrac{25}{4} = \tfrac{3}{4}$$

So f(x) written in completed square form is:

$$f(x) = \left(x + \tfrac{5}{2}\right)^2 + \tfrac{3}{4}$$

The bracket is <u>always</u>:
$$a\left(x + \frac{b}{2a}\right)^2$$

<u>Always</u> put:
bracket² + number = old expression for f(x).

The x² and x terms are the same on both sides so they cancel out. If they don't, you've got the bracket wrong.

You need to show that f(x)=0 has no roots.

$$f(x) = \left(x + \tfrac{5}{2}\right)^2 + \tfrac{3}{4} = 0$$

You'll need to write something like this to show that you understand why it has no roots. Otherwise you won't get the marks.

The squared bracket can <u>never</u> be less than 0. So the left-hand side can never be less than $\tfrac{3}{4}$. (So it can never be 0.) Therefore f(x) has <u>no roots</u>.

Paper 2 Q1 — Graphs and Integration

(iii) Sketching the **Graph** of y=f(x) — use the **Completed Square**

'Sketch the graph of f(x).' $f(x) = x^2 + 5x + 7 \implies y = x^2 + 5x + 7$

To draw the graph you need to know where it has max/min points and where it crosses the axes.

The coefficient of x^2 is <u>positive</u> (it's actually 1), so it's going to be a <u>u-shaped</u> graph (rather than n-shaped).

Find where the min occurs (use the completed square form):

$$f(x) = y = \left(x + \tfrac{5}{2}\right)^2 + \tfrac{3}{4}$$

The minimum of f(x) is when the squared bracket is 0.

So 3/4 is the minimum value, and occurs when x=−5/2.

<u>Where does it cross the axes?</u>
It's <u>not</u> going to cross the x-axis, because its minimum value is ¾.
We can find where it crosses the y-axis by putting x=0:

$$x = 0 \implies y = 7$$

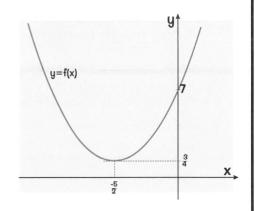

y=f(x)

7

3/4

−5/2

x

Evaluate the **Area** — Use Your **Sketch**

'Evaluate the area enclosed by the graph of f(x), the line $y = \frac{1}{\sqrt{2}}$, the line $x = \sqrt{2}$ and the y-axis.'

The first thing to do is to sketch the situation so you can see <u>exactly</u> what you've got to do.

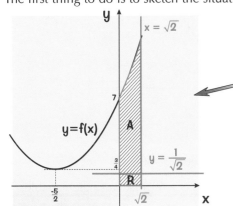

And draw on the 2 lines $x = \sqrt{2}$ and $y = \frac{1}{\sqrt{2}}$.

$\frac{1}{\sqrt{2}}$ is about 0.71, so it's just below $\frac{3}{4}$.

I've labelled two regions on the graph (A and R).
Area A is the region you need to find. R is the small rectangular region underneath it.

$$\text{area A} = \text{area A+R} - \text{area R}$$

Find this easily.

This is what we want.

Integrating y between 0 and $\sqrt{2}$ will give you the area A+R. (You find areas under curves by integrating. See pages 31-33.)

Find Area A+R:

$$\text{Area A+R} = \int_0^{\sqrt{2}} y\,dx = \int_0^{\sqrt{2}} (x^2 + 5x + 7)\,dx$$

$$= \left[\frac{x^3}{3} + \frac{5x^2}{2} + 7x\right]_0^{\sqrt{2}}$$

$$= \left(\frac{\sqrt{2}^3}{3} + \frac{5\sqrt{2}^2}{2} + 7\sqrt{2}\right) - \left(\frac{0^3}{3} + \frac{5\times 0^2}{2} + 7\times 0\right)$$

$$= \frac{2\sqrt{2}}{3} + \frac{5\times 2}{2} + 7\sqrt{2} \quad - \quad 0$$

$$= \sqrt{2}\left(\frac{2+21}{3}\right) + 5 = \frac{23}{3}\sqrt{2} + 5$$

Find Area R:

$$\text{Area R} = \text{length} \times \text{height} = \left(\sqrt{2} - 0\right) \times \left(\frac{1}{\sqrt{2}} - 0\right)$$

$$= \frac{\sqrt{2}}{\sqrt{2}} = 1$$

Find Area A:

$$\text{Area A} = \text{A+R} - \text{R}$$

$$= \frac{23}{3}\sqrt{2} + 5 - 1 = \frac{23}{3}\sqrt{2} + 4$$

Integrating graphs is an area that needs a lot of attention...

This is a pretty easy question, except for the last bit — and that's not <u>too</u> bad, once you've done the sketch. But if you've any sense, you'll check your answer... won't you. Your best bet with odd areas is to approximate it to easy shapes and check it's <u>about right</u>. For this question, it'd be a rectangle $\sqrt{2}$ by $\left(7 - \frac{1}{\sqrt{2}}\right)$ and a triangle $\sqrt{2}$ wide and roughly (16–7) tall.

Paper 2 Q2 — Trigonometry

2 **(i)** Sketch the graph of $y = \cos(x - 60°)$ for x between $0°$ and $360°$. [2]

(ii) Show that the equation $2\sin^2(x - 60°) = 1 + \cos(x - 60°)$
may be written as a quadratic in $\cos(x - 60°)$. [4]

(iii) Hence solve this equation, giving all values of x such that $0° \leq x \leq 360°$. [4]

(i) A **cos** graph shifted 60° to the **Right**

'Sketch the graph of $y = \cos(x - 60°)$ for x between $0°$ and $360°$.'

It's pretty easy to remember that you have to shift the graph <u>sideways</u> when the '−60°' is <u>inside</u> the brackets.
But what's not so easy is to remember which <u>direction</u> to shift it — to the <u>left</u> or to the <u>right</u>.

It'll help you decide which way to move the graph if you remember this:

$\cos x = 1$ when $x = 0$.
So $\cos(x - 60°) = 1$ when $x - 60° = 0$ — and this is when <u>$x = 60°$</u>.

> The graph is shifted horizontally by 60°. Because it's <u>minus</u> 60°, it's shifted to the <u>right</u>.

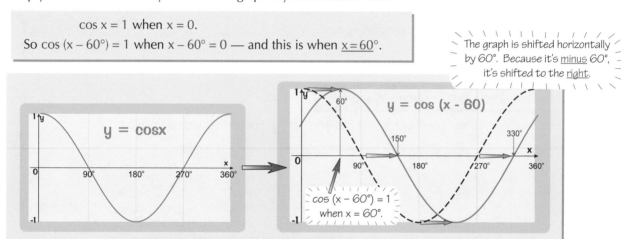

$\cos(x - 60°) = 1$ when $x = 60°$.

(ii) Use **sin² + cos² = 1** to get rid of the **sin²**

'Show that the equation $2\sin^2(x - 60°) = 1 + \cos(x - 60°)$ may be written as a quadratic in $\cos(x - 60°)$.'

'A quadratic in cos (x − 60°)...' — sounds a bit hard. But all you have to do is treat cos (x − 60°) like a single variable.

$$2\sin^2(x - 60°) = 1 + \cos(x - 60°) \quad \text{—①}$$

But 'sin² (anything)+cos² (anything) = 1'. With a little rearranging, this means you can <u>replace</u> the sin² with a 1 − cos².

You know from above that

$$2\sin^2(x - 60°) = 1 + \cos(x - 60°)$$

$$\sin^2(x-60°) + \cos^2(x-60°) = 1$$
$$\Rightarrow \sin^2(x-60°) = 1 - \cos^2(x-60°)$$

Now you can substitute for sin² (x − 60°) in this to give...

$$2\{1 - \cos^2(x - 60°)\} = 1 + \cos(x - 60°)$$

> You could even substitute y for x−60° — and work with sin²y and cos²y instead.

Now just multiply out the bracket and <u>rearrange</u> this so that everything's on one side.

$$2\{1 - \cos^2(x - 60°)\} = 1 + \cos(x - 60°)$$
$$\Rightarrow 2 - 2\cos^2(x - 60°) = 1 + \cos(x - 60°)$$
$$\Rightarrow 2\cos^2(x - 60°) + \cos(x - 60°) - 1 = 0$$

> If you write y = cos (x − 60°), then this is $2y^2 + y - 1 = 0$. That's what the question means by 'a quadratic in cos(x − 60°)'.

Paper 2 Q2 — Trigonometry

(iii) | It's a **Quadratic**, so try to **Factorise** it

'Hence solve this equation, giving all values of x such that $0° \leq x \leq 360°$.'

It's another question that looks a lot more frightening than it actually is. The most important thing is that you do it one bit at a time. You've got a quadratic equation (even though it's a horrible-looking one), so try to factorise it.

But it's probably a good idea to <u>rewrite</u> it a bit first so that it looks friendlier...

$$2\cos^2(x-60°) + \cos(x-60°) - 1 = 0$$

If you substitute y for cos(x – 60°), this becomes...

$$2y^2 + y - 1 = 0$$

> Yep, it's a normal quadratic, so try to factorise it — and if it won't factorise, use the quadratic formula.

This quadratic factorises to give...

$$(2y-1)(y+1) = 0$$
$$\Rightarrow y = \frac{1}{2} \quad \text{or} \quad y = -1$$

So you've found what y is. But y = cos(x – 60°), and so...

$$\cos(x-60°) = \frac{1}{2} \quad \text{or} \quad \cos(x-60°) = -1$$

> At this stage, alarm bells should definitely be ringing — you've just drawn the graph of y = cos(x – 60°), and you can use that to help solve this part.

And by taking the inverse cosine of these, you get...

$$x - 60° = \cos^{-1}\left(\frac{1}{2}\right) = 60°$$
$$\Rightarrow x = 120°$$

or

$$x - 60° = \cos^{-1}(-1) = 180°$$
$$\Rightarrow x = 240°$$

> Get these values from your calculator.

So far, you've got two solutions — but there might be <u>more</u>. It's time to have another look at the graph from part 1. That's basically why they asked you to draw it — to <u>help</u> you with this part.

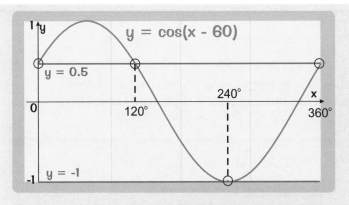

From equation 2, you know that you're looking for points where either:

$$\cos(x-60°) = \frac{1}{2} \quad \text{or} \quad \cos(x-60°) = -1.$$

Looking at the graph, there are <u>four</u> possible solutions — and you've already got two of them.

The other two solutions are at the extreme left and the extreme right, x = 0° and x = 360°.

So the four solutions are: x = 0°, x = 120°, x = 240° and x = 360°.

> All these solutions are okay since you have to find solutions with $0° \leq x \leq 360°$.

Get a tan — cos you're worth it...

What a question — what a pain. It relies on knowing all sorts of things: graphs, sin² + cos² = 1, solving quadratics, solving trig equations, and more besides. The thing to remember, though, is that with questions like this, later parts often make use of stuff you worked out in the earlier sections — so if something seems outrageously difficult, have a look at what you've already done and see if you can get a hint from that.

Paper 2 Q3 — Arc Length and Sector Area

3   A new symmetrical mini-stage is to be built according to the design shown below. The design consists of a rectangle of length q metres and width $2r$ metres, two sectors of radius r and angle θ radians (shaded), and an isoceles triangle.

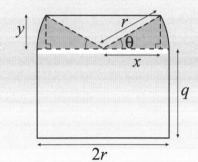

(i)   (a)   Show that distance x is given by $x = r\cos\theta$.   [2]

(b)   Find a similar expression for distance y.   [2]

(ii)   Find in terms of r, q and θ, expressions for the perimeter P, and the area A, of the stage.   [3]

(i) *Easy stuff with a **Right-Angled** triangle*

'Show that distance x is given by $x = r\cos\theta$ ...and find a similar expression for distance y.'

(a)   It's easier if you draw a <u>picture</u> of the thing you're interested in. Here, it's the triangle in the top-right corner. This is a <u>right-angled</u> triangle with an angle θ and hypotenuse r, and you need the length of the side <u>adjacent</u> to the angle — so use the cos formula...

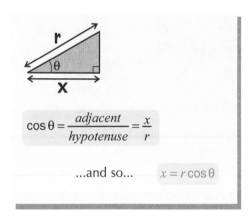

$$\cos\theta = \frac{adjacent}{hypotenuse} = \frac{x}{r}$$

...and so... $x = r\cos\theta$

(b)   The question says that the stage is <u>symmetrical</u>, so although y is marked on the left-hand side of the picture, you can use your picture of the right-hand side. Distance y is the side <u>opposite</u> the angle — so use the sine formula...

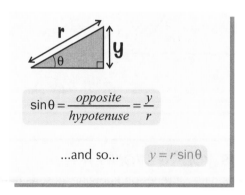

$$\sin\theta = \frac{opposite}{hypotenuse} = \frac{y}{r}$$

...and so... $y = r\sin\theta$

Paper 2 Q3 — Arc Length and Sector Area

(ii) Find the Areas of Sectors and lengths of Arcs

'Find in terms of r, q and θ, expressions for the perimeter P, and the area A, of the stage.'

Again, it helps if you draw a picture so you can get a better idea of what's going on.

Do the perimeter first: the red bits are easy — but you need the lengths S too.
Since the shaded areas are <u>sectors</u> of circles, use the formula for the length of an <u>arc</u>...

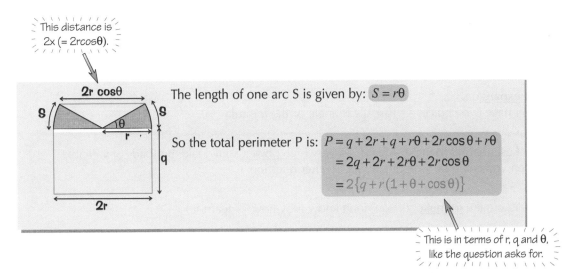

This distance is $2x\ (= 2r\cos\theta)$.

The length of one arc S is given by: $\boxed{S = r\theta}$

So the total perimeter P is: $\boxed{P = q + 2r + q + r\theta + 2r\cos\theta + r\theta}$

$= 2q + 2r + 2r\theta + 2r\cos\theta$

$= 2\{q + r(1 + \theta + \cos\theta)\}$

This is in terms of r, q and θ, like the question asks for.

Now do the same sort of thing for the area — break it down into easier lumps. The total area A is given by...

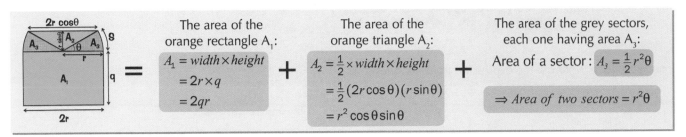

The area of the orange rectangle A_1:

$A_1 = width \times height$
$= 2r \times q$
$= 2qr$

$+$

The area of the orange triangle A_2:

$A_2 = \frac{1}{2} \times width \times height$
$= \frac{1}{2}(2r\cos\theta)(r\sin\theta)$
$= r^2 \cos\theta\sin\theta$

$+$

The area of the grey sectors, each one having area A_3:

Area of a sector: $\boxed{A_3 = \frac{1}{2}r^2\theta}$

$\Rightarrow Area\ of\ two\ sectors = r^2\theta$

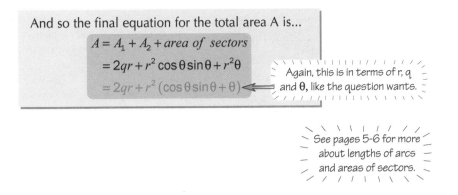

And so the final equation for the total area A is...

$A = A_1 + A_2 + area\ of\ sectors$

$= 2qr + r^2\cos\theta\sin\theta + r^2\theta$

$= 2qr + r^2(\cos\theta\sin\theta + \theta)$

Again, this is in terms of r, q and θ, like the question wants.

See pages 5-6 for more about lengths of arcs and areas of sectors.

For your information I lead a rich and varied social life...

Bit of a stinky question, that. It looks nasty when you first clap eyes on it, but as long as you keep your head and break it down into small, manageable chunks, it isn't really so bad. That's the way with a lot of these questions, but quite often the question guides you through what you're supposed to do — so one big, difficult question becomes a few smaller, easier questionettes. The moral of this story is then: don't panic if the question looks impossible when you first see the exam paper — it's probably not so bad when you get down to it. And if it's still bad when you get down to it, use the Force...

Paper 2 Q4 — Binomial Expansion

4 **(i)** Write down the first four terms in the expansion of $(1 + ax)^{10}$, $a > 0$. [2]

(ii) Find the coefficient of x^2 in the expansion of $(2 + 3x)^5$. [2]

(iii) If the coefficients of x^2 in both expansions are equal, find the value of a. [2]

(i) *Binomial Expansion — Use the Formula but watch out for the 'a'*

'Write down the first four terms in the expansion of $(1 + ax)^{10}$, $a > 0$.'

It's a <u>binomial expansion</u>.
That means you have two choices — Pascal's Triangle or the formula.

Now you *could* use Pascal's triangle — but it's a very <u>high power</u>, so it'd take up loads of valuable exam time when you could be worrying about another question.

So it's time to dig out the <u>formula</u>. (If you don't know it by now — learn it.)

There's more detail on the Binomial Expansion on page 28.

(1) Start by writing down the formula:

$$(1+x)^n = 1 + \frac{n}{1}x + \frac{n(n-1)}{1 \times 2}x^2 + \frac{n(n-1)(n-2)}{1 \times 2 \times 3}x^3 + \ldots\ldots + x^n$$

(2) Then write out the expression from the question...

$$(1 + ax)^{10}$$

Before you go any further, alarm bell should be ringing — you've got 'ax' instead of 'x'. Just remember that, OK.

(3) ...expand it...

$$= 1 + \frac{10}{1}(ax) + \frac{10 \times 9}{1 \times 2}(ax)^2 + \frac{10 \times 9 \times 8}{1 \times 2 \times 3}(ax)^3 + \ldots$$

REMEMBER — square / cube the WHOLE BRACKET, not just the 'x'

(4) ...and finally, simplify it.

$$= 1 + 10ax + \frac{90}{2}a^2x^2 + \frac{720}{6}a^3x^3 + \ldots$$

$$= 1 + 10ax + 45a^2x^2 + 120a^3x^3 + \ldots$$

So $(1 + ax)^{10}$ =  $1 + 10ax + 45a^2x^2 + 120a^2x^2 + \ldots$

Paper 2 Q4 — Binomial Expansion

(ii) Binomial Expansion again — Watch out for the '2'

'Find the coefficient of x^2 in the expansion of $(2 + 3x)^5$.'

(1) Again — start by writing down the formula:

$$(1+x)^n = 1 + \frac{n}{1}x + \frac{n(n-1)}{1\times 2}x^2 + \frac{n(n-1)(n-2)}{1\times 2 \times 3}x^3 + \ldots\ldots + x^n$$

(2) Then write out the expression from the question.

$$(2 + 3x)^5 \longleftarrow$$

> Again, look out. This time you've got a '2', not a '1', and you've got a '3x' instead of an 'x'.

(3) You have to take a factor of 2 out to get it in the form you want:

$$(2+3x)^5 = \left[2\left(1+\tfrac{3}{2}x\right)\right]^5$$
$$= 2^5 \left(1+\tfrac{3}{2}x\right)^5$$
$$= 32\left(1+\tfrac{3}{2}x\right)^5$$

> Remember to take the 2 to the power 5, not just the bracket.

(4) Then expand it as before (only up to the x^2 term this time):

$$32\left(1+\tfrac{3}{2}x\right)^5 = 32\left[1+\frac{5}{1}\left(\tfrac{3}{2}x\right)+\frac{5\times 4}{1\times 2}\left(\tfrac{3}{2}x\right)^2 + \ldots\right]$$

(5) You only need the x^2 term so just simplify that one:

$$x^2 \text{ term} = 32 \times \frac{5\times 4}{1\times 2}\left(\tfrac{3}{2}x\right)^2$$

> Cancel as much as you can to make the calculation easier.

$$= \frac{^{16}\cancel{32}\times \cancel{20}^5}{^1\cancel{2}}\times \frac{9}{\cancel{4}^{1}}x^2 = 16\times 5\times 9x^2 = 80\times 9x^2$$
$$= 720x^2$$

So the coefficient of the x^2 term is 720.

(iii) Equate coefficients from the first two answers — no problem

'If the coefficients of x^2 in both expansions are equal, find the value of a.'

If I was less of a cynic, I'd think they put in questions like this to be nice to you. But it's more likely they just put them in when they need a 2-mark question to make up the total marks. But whatever the reason, here's what you do:

The x^2 term from **(i)** was $45a^2x^2$ and the x^2 term from **(ii)** was $720x^2$

You're told that the coefficients are equal, so guess what you do...

...yep, you put them equal to each other! (genius) $\Longrightarrow$ $45a^2 = 720$

Then just fiddle around with it to solve for a: $\Longrightarrow$ $a^2 = 720 \div 45 = 16$

so $a = \pm 4$

But since it says in Question **(i)** that $a > 0$, you can confidently say that $a = 4$.

---

binomial expansion: $(1 - \text{binomial})^7 = 1 + 7\,\text{binomial} + 21\,\text{binomial}^2 + 35\,\text{binomial}^3 + \ldots$ ho ho

The problem with the binomial expansion is that it's a bit fiddly — there are loads of bits to it, and that means loads of opportunities for cocking it up. So the best advice I can give is to firstly *LEARN* the expansion, and secondly to take *EXTRA SPECIAL CARE* when using it. Check every step carefully until you're confident you haven't missed anything.

Paper 2 Q5 — Trapezium Rule

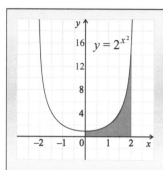

5   The diagram shows the graph of $y = 2^{x^2}$.

  (i) Use the trapezium rule with 4 intervals to find an estimate for the area of the region bounded by the axes, the curve and the line $x = 2$.   [4]

  (ii) State whether the estimate in (i) is an overestimate or an underestimate, giving a reason for your answer.   [2]

(i)   *Make a Rough Sketch of the Four Trapezia*

'Use the trapezium rule with 4 intervals to find an estimate for the area of the region bounded by the axes, the curve and the line $x = 2$.'

Drawing even a very rough sketch of the graph can help you see what you're actually doing.
Copy the graph and add on the 4 strips.
Here's one I made earlier:

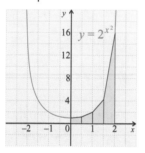

Look up the formula for the trapezium rule in the formula booklet and write it down:

$$\int_a^b y\, dx \approx \frac{h}{2}\big[y_0 + 2(y_1 + y_2 + \ldots + y_{n-1}) + y_n\big]$$

n is the number of intervals
h is the width of each strip

The width of each strip is 0.5 — you can get that from your sketch or by working out $h = \frac{2-0}{4} = 0.5$.

Draw up a table to work out the *y*-values.

x	$y = 2^{x^2}$
$x_0 = 0$	$y_0 = 2^{0^2} = 2^0 = 1$
$x_1 = 0.5$	$y_1 = 2^{0.5^2} = 2^{0.25} = 1.189$ (3 d.p.)
$x_2 = 1$	$y_2 = 2^{1^2} = 2^1 = 2$
$x_3 = 1.5$	$y_3 = 2^{1.5^2} = 2^{2.25} = 4.757$ (3 d.p.)
$x_4 = 2$	$y_4 = 2^{2^2} = 2^4 = 16$

Putting all these values into the formula gives:

$$\int_0^2 2^{x^2}\, dx \approx \frac{0.5}{2}\big[1 + 2(1.189 + 2 + 4.757) + 16\big]$$

$$= \frac{1}{4}(1 + 15.892 + 16)$$

$$= \frac{1}{4}(32.892)$$

$$= 8.22 \text{ (3 s.f.)}$$

As long as you're careful with all that working out, I'm sure you'll have no trouble.

Paper 2 Q5 — Trapezium Rule

(ii) *The shape of the curve tells you whether it's an overestimate or underestimate*

'State whether the estimate in (i) is an overestimate or an underestimate, giving a reason for your answer.'

Looking back at the sketch of the curve:

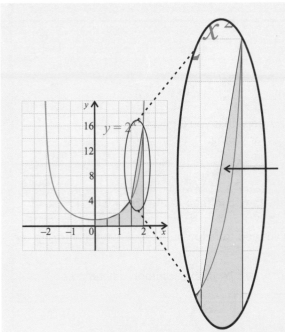

Each trapezium goes higher than the curve, so within each interval, the area of each trapezium is greater than the area under the curve.

The trapezium rule therefore gives an **overestimate** for the area.

Logarithm 'n' blues

Hate to do this to you, but I'm going to sneakily give you an extra question for practice... and it's on logs. I know, I know, I'm a wicked person, but I'm sure you'll rise to the challenge. It'll be over soon.

You can see on the graph of $y = 2^{x^2}$ that the line goes through the point (2, 16).

See if you can work backwards from $2^{x^2} = 16$, using logs, to show that $x = 2$ is a solution.

I'll give you a few seconds to think about it...

La la la, la la la-la la la la la, la la la-la la...   That's Kylie, by the way.

Right then.

Take logs of both sides (to the base 2 so you can bring that x^2 down):

Use the law of logs:

$$2^{x^2} = 16$$

$$\log_2 2^{x^2} = \log_2 16$$

$$x^2 \log_2 2 = \log_2 16 \quad \text{Spot that } \log_2 2 \text{ is 1 (because } 2^1 = 2).$$

$$x^2 = \log_2 16 \quad \text{Spot that } \log_2 16 \text{ is 4 (because } 2^4 = 16).$$

$$x^2 = 4$$

$$x = \pm 2 \quad \text{Remember the '}\pm\text{' — the graph is symmetrical about the y-axis.}$$

All over. See how clever you are? You can take anything I throw at you.

Paper 2 Q6 — Arithmetic Series

6 **(i)** An arithmetic series has first term a and common difference d.

Prove that the sum of the first n terms, S_n, is given by the formula $S_n = \frac{n}{2}[2a + (n-1)d]$. [4]

(ii) Evaluate $\sum_{n=9}^{32}(2n-5)$. [4]

(i)(a) Start by writing down the terms

'Prove that the sum of the first n terms, S_n, is given by the formula $S_n = \frac{n}{2}[2a + (n-1)d]$.'

There are 3 steps to proving this formula. They're not exactly steps that you'd guess but but as long as you remember what they are, you won't go far wrong.

Step 1: Write down the terms

Step 2: Write out 2 versions of the sum S_n

Step 3: Add together the sums from Step 2, do some cancelling and then fiddle about with it a bit.

The first thing you do is use the information the question gives you to help you <u>write down the terms in the series</u>. Make yourself a little table so you're clear what's going on...

You're told that the first term is a and that each term increases by d, the common difference.

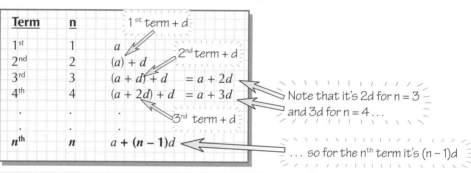

Term	n	
1st	1	a
2nd	2	$(a) + d$
3rd	3	$(a + d) + d \quad = a + 2d$
4th	4	$(a + 2d) + d \quad = a + 3d$
.	.	.
nth	n	$a + (n-1)d$

Each term is made up of the previous term plus d.

1st term + d
2nd term + d
3rd term + d

Note that it's 2d for n = 3 and 3d for n = 4 ...

... so for the nth term it's (n – 1)d

So to recap — the last term, which I'll call L, is: $L = a + (n-1)d$

(i)(b) Write down two versions of S_n

Now you've got to <u>use your table to build up the sum S_n</u>. S_n is the sum of the first n terms in you table. Here we go ...

Term 1	Term 2	Term 3	Term 4	. . .	Term n – 1	Term n
$n = 1$	$n = 2$	$n = 3$	$n = 4$	. . .	$n = n-1$	$n = n$
a	$a + d$	$a + 2d$	$a + 3d$	. . .	$L - d$	L

S_n is the sum of all these terms

L is the nth term. The term before the nth term will be an amount 'd' (the common difference) less than L

You can (and need to, for this question), write the sum the other way round — starting with the nth term and working back like this ...

Term n	Term n – 1	Term n – 2	. . .	Term 3	Term 2	Term 1
$n = n$	$n = n-1$	$n = n-2$	. . .	$n = 3$	$n = 2$	$n = 1$
L	$L - d$	$L - 2d$	. . .	$a + 2d$	$a + d$	a

S_n is also the sum of all these terms

Paper 2 Q6 — Arithmetic Series

(i)(c) | Then add them together and cancel most of the terms

Now for the tricky bit. Are you ready. . .

The easiest way to see the point of this is if you line up opposite terms in your two tables.
That is, line up the first term with the last, the second with the second last, and so on.

S_n forwards	$a + a+d + a+2d + a+3d + \ldots + L-3d + L-2d + L-d + L$
S_n backwards	$L + L-d + L-2d + L-3d + \ldots + a+3d + a+2d + a+d + a$

Take a minute and look closely at these. You'll see that if you add the two sums together all of
the d's cancel out — you're left with a simpler formula involving only a's and L's:

So,

$$2S_n = a + a+\cancel{d} + a+2\cancel{d} + a+3\cancel{d} + \ldots + L-3\cancel{d} + L-2\cancel{d} + L-\cancel{d} + L$$
$$+ L + L-\cancel{d} + L-2\cancel{d} + L-3\cancel{d} + \ldots + a+3\cancel{d} + a+2\cancel{d} + a+\cancel{d} + a$$

So if you take two sums of n terms and add them together,
you end up with n a-terms and n L-terms:

$$2S_n = na + nL$$

Using the formula for the last
term defined in part 1(a):

$$S_n = \frac{n}{2}(a + L)$$

$$L = a + (n-1)d \ldots$$

$$\Rightarrow S_n = \frac{n}{2}[2a + (n-1)d]$$

There are n terms in each sum. Half of the terms in each are a-terms and half are L-terms. Adding the sums together gives you n a-terms and n L-terms.

. . . and relax.

(ii) | Work out the sum of the entire series then subtract the first bit

'Evaluate $\displaystyle\sum_{n=9}^{32}(2n-5)$.'

Look at the top and bottom of the $\sum$ sign for the limits of the sum. The lower limit is at the bottom and the upper limit is at the top.

This part of the question is much easier. The $\displaystyle\sum_{n=9}^{32}$ sign is just a mathsey
way of asking you to work out a sum. Here, you're being
asked to work out $(2n-5)$ for all n values from 9 to 32, then add them up.

The easiest way to do this is to work out the whole sum (from the first to the 32nd term)
and then subtract the first 8 terms (the bit of the sum from $n = 1$ to $n = 8$).

All you need to do here is plug the a, n and L values into the equation from part (i):
$$S_n = \frac{n}{2}(a+L) \text{, and you're laughing.}$$

L, the last term, in the whole sum is 2n − 5 for n = 32

$$\sum_{n=9}^{n=32}(2n-5) = \sum_{n=1}^{n=32}(2n-5) - \sum_{n=1}^{n=8}(2n-5)$$

$$= \frac{32}{2}\left\{[(2\times1)-5]+[(2\times32)-5]\right\} - \frac{8}{2}\left\{[(2\times1)-5]+[(2\times8)-5]\right\}$$

$$= \frac{32(-3+59)}{2} - \frac{8(-3+11)}{2}$$

$$= 896 - 32$$

$$= 864$$

L, the last term, in the first eight terms is 2n − 5 for n = 8

Now could you dream of a better question in your exam... (shudder)

Now either learn that method or pray it doesn't come up . . .

To be honest, I think they'd be a bit mean to give you a question like that — but thought I'd better put it in,
just in case. Because it's pretty easy if you remember the trick... and darned near impossible otherwise.

Paper 2 Q7 — Geometric Series

7 A geometric series $u_1 + u_2 + ... + u_n$ has 3rd term $\frac{5}{2}$ and 6th term $\frac{5}{16}$.

(i) Find the common ratio and the first term of the series. Hence give the formula for the nth term of the series. [4]

(ii) Find $\sum\limits_{n=1}^{10} u_n$. Give your answer as a fraction in its simplest terms. [3]

(iii) Show that the sum to infinity of the series is 20. [2]

(i) Put the numbers they give you into the Formula for the nth Term

'Find the common ratio and the first term of the series.'

So far, you've only got a couple of bits of information. You know:

(i) that this is a <u>geometric</u> series,

and   (ii) two of the terms.

So you might as well start by putting these values into the formula for the nth term.

> The formula for the nth term of a geometric series is:
> $$u_n = ar^{n-1}$$
> And substituting the values for u_3 and u_6 in this gives:
> $$u_3 = ar^2 = \frac{5}{2} \qquad u_6 = ar^5 = \frac{5}{16}$$

You need to find values for a and r from these two equations. That means you have to find some way of getting rid of either a or r — then you'll be able to find the value of the one that's left.

The trick here is to <u>divide</u> these two expressions, then you'll be able to <u>cancel</u> the a on the top and bottom lines.

Divide the expressions for u_3 and u_6...

Cancel the a, and also an r^2, to leave just r^3. → $\dfrac{ar^5}{ar^2} = r^3 = \dfrac{5/16}{5/2}$ ← An equation with just one unknown in it — r.

Now that you've got an equation just containing r, you can solve it.

$$r^3 = \frac{5/16}{5/2} = \frac{5}{16} \times \frac{2}{5} = \frac{5^1}{16^8} \cdot \frac{2^1}{5^1} = \frac{1}{8}$$

Cancel anything you can to make things easier.

So take the cube root, and you find...

$$r = \sqrt[3]{\frac{1}{8}} = \frac{1}{\sqrt[3]{8}} = \frac{1}{2}$$

See pages 25 – 27 for more about geometric series.

Substitute this value back into the equation for u_3 to find a...

$$ar^2 = \frac{5}{2}$$

You could use the equation for u_6, but this'll be easier because the power of r is smaller.

$$\Rightarrow a\left(\frac{1}{2}\right)^2 = \frac{1}{4}a = \frac{5}{2}$$
$$\Rightarrow a = 10$$

The hard work's done, you've found a and r — but the question asks you for the <u>formula for the nth term of the series</u>.

The nth term is given by $u_n = ar^{n-1}$, where $a = 10$ and $r = \frac{1}{2}$.

So,

$$u_n = 10 \cdot \left(\frac{1}{2}\right)^{n-1} = 10 \cdot \frac{1}{2^{n-1}} = \frac{10}{2^{n-1}}$$

Write your answer as simply as you can.

CHECK YOUR ANSWER:

You can check that your answer gives the numbers in the question.

Using $u_n = \dfrac{10}{2^{n-1}}$

$$u_3 = \frac{10}{2^2} = \frac{10}{4} = \frac{5}{2}$$

...so this one's okay. And

$$u_6 = \frac{10}{2^5} = \frac{10}{32} = \frac{5}{16}$$

...so this is fine too.

Paper 2 Q7 — Geometric Series

(ii) Now you need the *Sum* of the first *Ten Terms*

'Find $\displaystyle\sum_{n=1}^{10} u_n$.'

The Σ-notation just means that you're looking for a <u>sum</u> — so use the formula for the sum of the first n terms...

The sum of the first n terms of a <u>geometric series</u> is given by:

$$\sum_{i=1}^{n} u_i = S_n = \frac{a(1 - r^n)}{1 - r}$$

So put n = 10 to find the sum of the first ten terms, S_{10}...

$$S_{10} = \sum_{i=1}^{10} u_i = \frac{a(1 - r^{10})}{1 - r}$$

Then plug in the values you found for a and r in part (i)...

Using the values a = 10 and r = $\frac{1}{2}$ ...

$$S_{10} = 10 \times \frac{1 - \left(\frac{1}{2}\right)^{10}}{1 - \frac{1}{2}} = 10 \times \frac{1 - \frac{1}{2^{10}}}{\frac{1}{2}} = 10 \times 2 \times \left(1 - \frac{1}{2^{10}}\right)$$

Dividing by $\frac{1}{2}$ is the same as multiplying by 2.

Now simplify this as much as you can...

$$S_{10} = 20 \times \left(1 - \frac{1}{1024}\right) = 20 \times \left(\frac{1023}{1024}\right) = 5 \times \left(\frac{1023}{256}\right)$$

$$= \frac{5115}{256}$$

$2^{10} = 1024$

Cancelling a factor of 4 in both 20 and 1024.

There are no more common factors, so this is your final answer.

You can tell if a fraction can be cancelled down further by looking at the <u>prime factors</u> of the top and bottom lines.

E.g. $\dfrac{5115}{256} = \dfrac{5115}{2^8}$

1) The bottom line is 2^8, so the <u>only</u> factors you could possibly cancel are 2, 4, 8, 16,... and so on.

2) As 2 doesn't go into 5115, neither do 4, 8, 16,... etc. — so there are no common factors to cancel down.

(iii) And lastly, the *Sum to Infinity*

'Show that the sum to infinity of the series is 20.'

One bit to go, and they've told you what the answer should be — a comforting little check.

It's the sum to infinity this time — and that's easier than the previous bit.

The sum to infinity is given by...

$$S_\infty = \frac{a}{1 - r}$$

This only works if −1 < r < 1.

So using the values a = 10 and r = $\frac{1}{2}$ ...

$$S_\infty = \frac{10}{1 - \frac{1}{2}} = \frac{10}{\frac{1}{2}} = 10 \times 2 = 20$$

And that's handy, because it's the figure you're supposed to end up with.

IF YOU <u>DON'T</u> GET THE RIGHT ANSWER...

1) Check you haven't 'lost' any <u>minus signs</u> anywhere,

2) Make sure you've done any divisions involving fractions properly,

3) Check you've <u>copied</u> things down correctly from one line to the next.

If you really can't find your mistake, do another question and come back to this one <u>later</u> if you've got time.

Summertime... and the adding is easy...

There's really not that much they can ask you about geometric series — but they can dress the same stuff up in lots of different ways. Basically if you know three things: the formula for the nth term, the formula for the sum of the first n terms, and the formula for the sum to infinity, then you should be pretty well prepared to answer anything. One thing that's really important (and I mean REALLY important) is that you get used to deciding whether a series is arithmetic or geometric. For an <u>arithmetic</u> series, you <u>add</u> a number each time — and 'Arithmetic' and 'Add' both start with 'a'. For a <u>geometric</u> series, you <u>multiply</u> by a number each time — and 'Geometric' and 'Multiply' start with, er... 'g' and 'm'.

Paper 2 Q8 — Integration

8 (i) **(a)** Show that the graph of $f(x) = -x^2(x-2)$ has turning points at the origin and the point $\left(\frac{4}{3}, \frac{32}{27}\right)$. [3]

(b) Sketch the graph of $f(x)$, marking in any turning points and points where it crosses the axes. [2]

(ii) The function $g(x)$ is defined by $g(x) = 2 - x$. Given that the graphs of $f(x)$ and $g(x)$ meet at $x = 1$, sketch the graph of $g(x)$ on the same set of axes you used in part (i), marking in the coordinates of the two points of intersection for which x is positive. [3]

(iii) Show that the area enclosed by the two graphs between $x = 1$ and $x = 2$ is $\frac{5}{12}$. [3]

(i)(a) Differentiate — and then set the derivative equal to Zero

'Show that the graph of $f(x) = -x^2(x-2)$ has turning points at the origin and the point $\left(\frac{4}{3}, \frac{32}{27}\right)$.'

Turning points occur when $f'(x) = 0$. So first differentiate $f(x)$, then set the derivative to zero.

$$f(x) = -x^2(x-2)$$
$$= -x^3 + 2x^2$$

And so
$$f'(x) = -3x^2 + 2(2x^1)$$

Using the fact that $\frac{d}{dx}(x^n) = nx^{n-1}$.

$$= -3x^2 + 4x$$

$$= x(-3x + 4)$$

Factorise this so it's easy to see when it's zero.

Now put f'(x) equal to 0:

$$f'(x) = 0 \quad \Rightarrow \quad x(-3x + 4) = 0$$
$$\Rightarrow \quad x = 0 \quad \text{or} \quad x = \frac{4}{3}$$

So there are turning points at $x = 0$ and $x = \frac{4}{3}$.

But the question asks for the actual points, so you need to find the y-coordinates too, i.e. $f(0)$ and $f\left(\frac{4}{3}\right)$:

$$f(0) = 0, \text{ and } f\left(\frac{4}{3}\right) = -\left(\frac{4}{3}\right)^2\left(\frac{4}{3} - 2\right) = -\frac{16}{9}\left(-\frac{2}{3}\right) = \frac{32}{27}.$$

So the turning points are $(0,0)$ (i.e. the origin) and $\left(\frac{4}{3}, \frac{32}{27}\right)$.

(i)(b) Sketching f(x) — it's a Cubic

'Sketch the graph of $f(x)$, marking in any turning points and points where it crosses the axes.'

$$f(x) = -x^2(x-2) = -x^3 + 2x^2$$

There's basically three things you need to know to draw this graph:

1. What shape is the graph?

   f(x) is a cubic function, and the coefficient of x^3 is negative (–1) — so it goes from top-left to bottom-right.

2. Where does it cross the x-axis?

   Just put f(x) equal to 0:

3. Where are the turning points?

   We already know these from part i(a). Don't forget to mark them on.

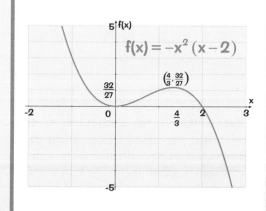

Paper 2 Q8 — Integration

(ii) | Sketch a **Straight** line on the **Same** pair of axes

'$g(x)$ is defined by $g(x) = 2 - x$. Given that the graphs of $f(x)$ and $g(x)$ meet at $x = 1$, sketch the graph of $g(x)$ on the same set of axes you used in part (i), marking in the coordinates of the two points of intersection for which x is positive.'

You've got to stick g(x), which is just a straight line, on your graph.
So all you do is <u>plot</u> 2 points and draw a straight line through them.
The best points to choose are where it <u>crosses</u> the x- and y- axes.

g(x) crosses the: <u>y-axis</u> at y = 2 (just put x = 0),
and the <u>x-axis</u> at x = 2 (just set g(x) = 0).

The question asks you to mark on the 2 points where f(x) and g(x) meet.

It tells you that they meet at x=1. And since $f(1) = -1^2(1-2) = 1$,
the two graphs cross at the point (1,1).
You can see the other point just by looking at the graph. It's (2,0).

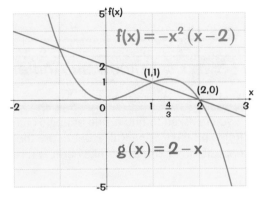

(iii) | Find the **Area** between the two lines

'Show that the area enclosed by the two graphs between $x = 1$ and $x = 2$ is $\frac{5}{12}$.'

Without a <u>graph</u>, this part of the question would be pretty tricky — but with the graph you drew in part (ii), you can see exactly which area you need to find. It also helps you to see <u>how</u> you need to go about finding it.

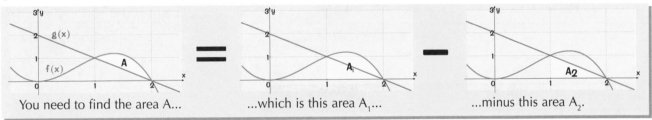

You need to find the area A...   ...which is this area A_1...   ...minus this area A_2.

To find areas under curves, you need to <u>integrate</u>. So...

Area A_1 is:
$$A_1 = \int_1^2 (-x^3 + 2x^2)\,dx$$
$$= \left[-\frac{x^4}{4} + \frac{2x^3}{3} \right]_1^2$$
$$= \left(-\frac{2^4}{4} + \frac{2 \times 2^3}{3} \right) - \left(-\frac{1^4}{4} + \frac{2 \times 1^3}{3} \right)$$
$$= \left(-4 + \frac{16}{3} \right) - \left(-\frac{1}{4} + \frac{2}{3} \right) = \frac{-48+64+3-8}{12} = \frac{11}{12}$$

$$\int_1^2 x^n \, dx = \left[\frac{x^{n+1}}{n+1} \right]_1^2$$

Never rush this bit as it's easy to lose a minus sign.

Or you could do it this way:
$$A = \int_1^2 \left[(-x^3 + 2x^2) - (2-x) \right] dx$$
See page 34 for more info.

The area A_2 is a <u>triangle</u>, and the quickest way to find its area is to use the formula: $Area = \frac{1}{2} base \times height$.

And the area A_2 is:
$$A_2 = \frac{1}{2} \times 1 \times 1$$
$$= \frac{1}{2}$$

You could integrate to find the area under the straight line — but this is quicker and easier.

And the area you need is just $A_1 - A_2$:

So the area <u>enclosed</u> by the curves between $x = 1$ and $x = 2$ is:
$$A = A_1 - A_2$$
$$= \frac{11}{12} - \frac{1}{2} = \frac{11-6}{12} = \frac{5}{12}$$

I've got a bad feeling about this...

This is a real meaty question, which makes it look horrendous — but a quick think and a quick sketch before you start will be dead useful (for part (iii) especially). And as long as you've had plenty of practice with the little tricks you need to use (e.g. differentiating to find turning points, sketching graphs, integrating to finding areas under graphs), you'll be all right.

Paper 2 Q9 — Sine and Cosine Rules

9 **(i)** Find the missing length a in the triangle. [4]

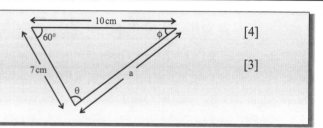

(ii) Find the angles θ and φ. [3]

(i) If you only know an **Angle** and the **Sides next to it**, use the **Cosine Rule**

'Find the missing length a...'

If you're asked to find a side or angle of a triangle without a right angle, there are two things you can try — the <u>Sine Rule</u> and the <u>Cosine Rule</u>. But to use the Sine Rule, you need to know both an angle and the length of the side opposite it. If you don't (like here), it'll have to be the Cosine Rule.

Use the Cosine Rule: $a^2 = b^2 + c^2 - 2bc \cos A$, putting b=10, c=7 and the angle A=60°.

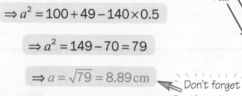

Remember: Side a is opposite angle A, and so on.

$$a^2 = b^2 + c^2 - 2bc \cos A$$

$$a^2 = 10^2 + 7^2 - 2 \times 10 \times 7 \times \cos 60°$$

$$\Rightarrow a^2 = 100 + 49 - 140 \times 0.5$$

There's nothing really that tricky in the Cosine Rule — just loads of fiddly stuff all stuck together.

$$\Rightarrow a^2 = 149 - 70 = 79$$

$$\Rightarrow a = \sqrt{79} = 8.89 \, cm$$

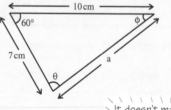

Don't forget the units.

It doesn't matter which side you choose to be b or c. Just stick to whatever you do choose.

(ii) Use the **Sine Rule** to find the missing angles

You've found side a in the first part of the question — so you know an angle and the length of the side opposite. Time to use the <u>Sine Rule</u> then. Don't worry — it's easier than falling off a dog.

'Find the angles θ...'

Now *θ* is the angle opposite the 10 cm side, and I called the 10 cm side b. So in the Sine Rule, *θ* is the angle B.

Put the values you know into the Sine Rule.

$$\frac{a}{\sin A} = \frac{b}{\sin B}$$

$$\frac{\sqrt{79}}{\sin 60°} = \frac{10}{\sin B}$$

Take sin B over to the left, and everything else to the right.

$$\Rightarrow \sin B = \frac{10 \times \sin 60°}{\sqrt{79}} = 0.974$$

$$\Rightarrow B = \sin^{-1} 0.9744 = 77.0°$$

Try to keep the full decimal answers on your calculator throughout the calculation. You should only actually round your answer at the very end.

The <u>Sine Rule</u>: In <u>any</u> triangle,

$$\frac{a}{\sin A} = \frac{b}{\sin B} = \frac{c}{\sin C}$$

The <u>Cosine Rule</u>: In <u>any</u> triangle,

$$a^2 = b^2 + c^2 - 2bc \cos A$$

'...and φ.'

Do exactly what you've just done. But use side c instead of b.

Put the values you know into the sine rule.

$$\frac{a}{\sin A} = \frac{c}{\sin C}$$

Rearrange things a bit.

And again — take the inverse sine to find the angle.

$$\Rightarrow \sin C = \frac{7 \times \sin 60°}{\sqrt{79}} = 0.6820$$

$$\Rightarrow C = \sin^{-1} 0.6820 = 43.0°$$

(Or you could just subtract the 2 angles you know from 180° — which is a good check.)

The Sine and Cosine Rules — I know what you're thinking...

The Sine and Cosine Rules are pretty darn easy, let's face it. If you get a question in the exam on them, you should be jumping for joy. They're both really flexible — for a triangle ABC, you could use any of these for the Cosine Rule: $a^2 = b^2 + c^2 - 2bc \sin A$, $b^2 = a^2 + c^2 - 2ac \sin B$, $c^2 = a^2 + b^2 - 2ab$. And for the Sine Rule, you can <u>either</u> put the lengths or the sine bits on the top:

So either write it $\frac{a}{\sin A} = \frac{b}{\sin B} = \frac{c}{\sin C}$ or $\frac{\sin A}{a} = \frac{\sin B}{b} = \frac{\sin C}{c}$. Wow!

Answers

Section One — Algebra and Functions

1) a) $(x^2 + 5x + 4)$ with 7 remainder

  b) $(-2x^2 + 4x - 8)$ with 18 remainder

2) a) $f(x) = (x + 2)(3x^2 - 10x + 15) - 36$

  b) $f(x) = (x + 2)(x^2 - 3) + 10$

3) a) (i) You just need to find $f(-1)$. This is $-6 - 1 + 3 - 12 = -16$.

  (ii) Now find $f(1)$. This is $6 - 1 - 3 - 12 = -10$.

  b) (i) $f(-1) = -1$

  (ii) $f(1) = 9$

4) Put $x = -2$. $x^3 + 5x^2 + 2x - 8 = -8 + 20 - 4 - 8 = 0$

  So by the Factor Theorem, $(x + 2)$ is a factor.

5) a) $(3x - 1)$ Put $x = \frac{1}{3}$ $\Rightarrow 3x^3 + 23x^2 + 37x - 15$

$$= \frac{3}{27} + \frac{23}{9} + \frac{37}{3} - 15$$

$$= \frac{135}{9} - 15 = 0$$

  so by the Factor Theorem, $\left(x - \frac{1}{3}\right)$ is a factor

  and so $(3x - 1)$ must be a factor too.

  b) $f(x) = (x - 1)(x - 2)(x + 2)$

6) If $f(x) = 2x^4 + 3x^3 + 5x^2 + cx + d$, then to make sure $f(x)$ is exactly divisible by $(x - 2)(x + 3)$, you have to make sure $f(2) = f(-3) = 0$.

  $f(2) = 32 + 24 + 20 + 2c + d = 0$, i.e. $\underline{2c + d = -76}$.

  $f(-3) = 162 - 81 + 45 - 3c + d = 0$, i.e. $\underline{3c - d = 126}$.

  Add the two underlined equations to get: $5c = 50$, and so $\underline{c = 10}$.

  Then $\underline{d = -96}$.

Section Two — Trigonometry

£100 See page 7

£200 See page 6

£300 See page 7

£500 **a)** $B=125°$, $a=3.66$ m, $c=3.10$ m, area is 4.64 m²

  b) $r=20.05$ km, $P=1.49°$, $Q=168.51°$

£1000 Freda's angles are $22.3°$, $49.5°$, $108.2°$

£2000 One triangle: $c=4.98$, $C=72.07°$, $B=72.93°$

  Other possible triangle: $c=3.22$, $C=37.93°$, $B=107.07°$

£4000 See page 9

£8000

  a)

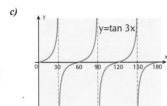

  b)

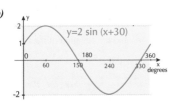

  c)

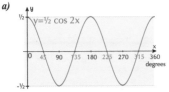

£16 000 **a)** $q = 240°$, $300°$.

  b) $q = 135°$, $315°$.

  c) $q = 135°$, $225°$.

£32 000 **a)** $q = 33.0°$, $57.0°$, $123.0°$, $147.0°$,

  $-33.0°$, $-57.0°$, $-123.0°$, $-147.0°$

  b) $q = -17.5°$, $127.5°$

  c) $q = 179.8°$

£64 000 $x = 70.5°$, $120°$, $240°$, $289.5°$.

£125 000 $x = -30°$

£250 000

$$(\sin y + \cos y)^2 + (\cos y - \sin y)^2$$

$$\equiv (\sin^2 y + 2\sin y \cos y + \cos^2 y) + (\cos^2 y - 2\cos y \sin y + \sin^2 y)$$

$$\equiv 2(\sin^2 y + \cos^2 y) \equiv 2$$

£500 000

$$\frac{\sin^4 x + \sin^2 x \cos^2 x}{\cos^2 x - 1} \equiv -1$$

LHS:

$$\equiv \frac{\sin^2 x (\sin^2 x + \cos^2 x)}{(1 - \sin^2 x) - 1}$$

$$\equiv \frac{\sin^2 x}{-\sin^2 x} \equiv -1 \equiv \text{RHS}$$

£1 million D is the correct answer.

Section Three — Logs and Exponentials

1) a) $3^3 = 27$ so $\log_3 27 = 3$

  b) to get fractions you need negative powers

  $3^{-3} = \frac{1}{27}$

  $\log_3 (\frac{1}{27}) = -3$

  c) logs are subtracted so divide

  $\log_3 18 - \log_3 2 = \log_3 (18 \div 2)$

  $= \log_3 9$

  $= 2$ $\quad (3^2 = 9)$

2) a) logs are added so you multiply — remember $2 \log 5 = \log 5^2$

  $\log 3 + 2 \log 5 = \log (3 \times 5^2)$

  $= \log 75$

  b) logs are subtracted so you divide and the power half means square root

  $\frac{1}{2} \log 36 - \log 3 = \log (36^{\frac{1}{2}} \div 3)$

  $= \log (6 \div 3)$

  $= \log 2$

3) This only looks tricky because of the algebra, just remember the laws

  $\log_b (\chi^2 - 1) - \log_b (\chi - 1) = \log_b \{(\chi^2 - 1)/(\chi - 1)\}$

  using the difference of two squares $(\chi^2 - 1) = (\chi - 1)(\chi + 1)$ and cancelling

  $= \log_b (\chi + 1)$

4) a) Filling in the answers is just a case of using the calculator

x	-3	-2	-1	0	1	2	3
y	0.0156	0.0625	0.25	1	4	16	64

  Check that it agrees with what we know about the graphs. It goes through the common point (0,1), and it follows the standard shape.

  b) Then you just need to draw the graph, and use a scale that's just right.

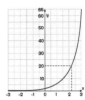

  c) The question tells you to use the graph to get your answer, so you'll need to include the construction lines, but check the answer with the calculator.

  $x = \log 20 / \log 4 = 2.16$, but you can't justify this accuracy if your graph's not up to it, so 2.2 is a good estimate.

Answers

5) a) $x > \dfrac{4}{3}$

b) $x < -\dfrac{3}{4}$

6) a) $x = \log_{10}240 / \log_{10}10 = \log_{10}240 = 2.380$

b) $x = 10^{2.6} = 398.1$

c) $2x + 1 = \log_{10}1500 = 3.176$, so $2x = 2.176$, so $x = 1.088$

d) $(x - 1) \log 4 = \log 200$, so $x - 1 = \log200 / \log4 = 3.822$, so $x = 4.822$

7) First solve for $1.5^P = 1,000,000$
$P \times \log_{10}1.5 = \log_{10}1,000,000$,
so $P = (\log_{10}1,000,000) / (\log_{10}1.5) = 34.07$.
We need the next biggest integer, so this will be $P = 35$.

Section Four — Sequences and Series

1) a) $u_1 = 1^2 + 3 = 4$; $u_2 = 2^2 + 3 = 7$; $u_3 = 3^2 + 3 = 12$;
$u_4 = 4^2 + 3 = 19$

b) $u_{20} = 20^2 + 3 = 403$

2) $x_2 = 3 \times 4 - 2 = 10$; $x_3 = 3 \times 10 - 2 = 28$; $x_4 = 3 \times 28 - 2 = 82$

3) Solve $L = 3L/4 + 7$, i.e. $L/4 = 7$, i.e. $L = 28$

4) $a = 5, d = 3, l = 65$
$a + (n - 1)d = l$
$5 + 3(n - 1) = 65$
$3(n - 1) = 60$
$n - 1 = 20$
$n = 21$

$S_{21} = 21(\dfrac{5+65}{2}) = 735$

5) a) $a + (n - 1)d = $ nth term
$7 + (5 - 1)d = 23$
$4d = 16$
$d = 4$

b) $a + (15 - 1)d$ is 15th term
$= a + 14d = 7 + 14 \times 4 = 63$

c) $S_{10} = \dfrac{10}{2}[2 \times 7 + (10 - 1) \times 4]$

$S_{10} = 5(14 + 36) = 250$

6) $a + 6d = 36$
$a + 9d = 30$
Subtract one equation from the other:
$-3d = 6$
$d = -2$
Plug d into one of the original equations:
$a + 6 \times -2 = 36$
$a - 12 = 36$
$a = 48$

$S_5 = \dfrac{5}{2}[2 \times 48 + (5 - 1) \times -2]$

$S_5 = \dfrac{5}{2}(96 - 8) = 220$

n^{th} term $= a + (n - 1)d$
$= 48 + (n - 1) \times -2$
$= 48 - 2n + 2 = 50 - 2n$

7) a) $\displaystyle\sum_{n=1}^{20}(3n - 1) = 2 + 5 + 8 + ... + 59 = 20(\dfrac{2+59}{2}) = 610$

b) $\displaystyle\sum_{n=1}^{10}(48 - 5n) = 43 + 38 + 33 + ... + -2 = 10(\dfrac{43+-2}{2}) = 205$

8) $a = 2, r = -3$
10th term, $u_{10} = ar^9$
$= 2 \times (-3)^9 = -39366$

9) a) $r = $ 2nd term $\div$ 1st term
$r = 12 \div 24 = \frac{1}{2}$

b) 7th term $= ar^6$
$= 24 \times (\frac{1}{2})^6$
$= 0.375$ (or $\frac{3}{8}$)

c) $S_\infty = \dfrac{a}{1 - r} = \dfrac{24}{1 - \frac{1}{2}} = 48$

10) **G.P.** — 2, 6, ... $a = 2, r = 3$
5th term is $ar^4 = 2 \times 3^4 = \underline{162}$
A.P. — 2, 6, ... $a = 2, d = 4$
You need $a + (n - 1)d = 162$
$2 + (n - 1)4 = 162$
$4(n - 1) = 160$
$n - 1 = 40$
$\underline{n = 41}$ i.e. the 41st term of the AP is equal to the 5th term of the G.P.

11) $(2 + 3x)^5 = 2^5(1 + \dfrac{3}{2}x)^5$

$= 2^5[1 + \dfrac{5}{1}(\dfrac{3}{2}x) + \dfrac{5 \times 4}{1 \times 2}(\dfrac{3}{2}x)^2 + ...]$

x^2 term is $2^5 \times \dfrac{5 \times 4}{1 \times 2}(\dfrac{3}{2})^2 x^2$, so coefficient is $2^5 \times \dfrac{5 \times 4}{1 \times 2} \times \dfrac{3^2}{2^2} = 720$

Section Five — Integration

1) i) Increase the power of x by 1, ii) divide by the new power, iii) add a constant.
This doesn't work for $x^{-1} = 1/x$.

2) An integral without limits to integrate between. Because there's more than one right answer.

3) Differentiate your answer, and if you get back the function you integrated in the first place, your answer's right.

4) a) $2x^5 + C$

b) $-\dfrac{2}{x^2} + C$

c) $\dfrac{3}{4}x^4 + \dfrac{2}{3}x^3 + C$

d) $3x^{\frac{4}{3}} + C = 3\sqrt[3]{x^4} + C$

e) $x^6 + \dfrac{2}{x} + \dfrac{2}{3}x^{\frac{3}{2}} + C$

5) Integrating gives $y = 3x^2 - 7x + C$; then substitute $x=1$ and $y=0$ to find that $C = 4$. So the equation of the curve is $y = 3x^2 - 7x + 4$.

6) Integrate to get $y = \dfrac{2}{3}x^{\frac{3}{2}} - \dfrac{2}{x} + C$. Putting $x=1$ and $y=0$ gives $C = \frac{4}{3}$, and so the required curve is $y = \dfrac{2}{3}x^{\frac{3}{2}} - \dfrac{2}{x} + \dfrac{4}{3}$.
If the curve has to go through $(1, 2)$ instead of $(1, 0)$, substitute the values $x=1$ and $y=2$ to find a different value for C, call this value C_1.
Making these substitutions gives $C_1 = \dfrac{10}{3}$, and the equation of the new curve is $y = \dfrac{2}{3}x^{\frac{3}{2}} - \dfrac{2}{x} + \dfrac{10}{3}$.

7) Check whether there are limits to integrate between. If there are, then it's a definite integral; if not, it's an indefinite integral.

8) The area bounded by the curve, the appropriate axis and the two limits.

Answers

9) a) $\int_{-3}^{3}\left(9-x^2\right)dx = \left[9x - \dfrac{x^3}{3}\right]_{-3}^{3} = 18-(-18) = 36$

b) $\int_{1}^{\infty}\dfrac{3}{x^2}dx = \left[-\dfrac{3}{x}\right]_{1}^{\infty} = 0-(-3) = 3$

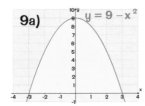

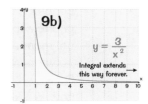

10) a) $\int_{0}^{1}\left(4x^3+3x^2+2x+1\right)dx$

$= \left[x^4+x^3+x^2+x\right]_{0}^{1}$

$= 4-0 = 4$

b) $\int_{1}^{2}\left(\dfrac{8}{x^5}+\dfrac{3}{\sqrt{x}}\right)dx = \left[-\dfrac{2}{x^4}+6\sqrt{x}\right]_{1}^{2}$

$= \left(-\dfrac{2}{16}+6\sqrt{2}\right)-(-2+6) = -\dfrac{33}{8}+6\sqrt{2}$

c) $\int_{1}^{6}\dfrac{3}{x^2}dx = \left[-\dfrac{3}{x}\right]_{1}^{6} = -\dfrac{1}{2}-(-3) = \dfrac{5}{2}$

11) a) $A = \int_{0}^{2}\left(x^3-5x^2+6x\right)dx$

$= \left[\dfrac{x^4}{4}-\dfrac{5}{3}x^3+3x^2\right]_{0}^{2} = \dfrac{8}{3}$

b) $A = \int_{1}^{4}2\sqrt{x}\,dx = \left[\dfrac{4}{3}x^{\frac{3}{2}}\right]_{1}^{4} = \dfrac{28}{3}$

c) $A = \int_{0}^{2}2x^2dx + \int_{2}^{6}(12-2x)dx$

$= \left[\dfrac{2}{3}x^3\right]_{0}^{2} + \left[12x-x^2\right]_{2}^{6}$

$= \dfrac{16}{3}+16 = \dfrac{64}{3}$

d) $A = \int_{1}^{4}(x+3)dx - \int_{1}^{4}\left(x^2-4x+7\right)dx$

$= \left[\dfrac{x^2}{2}+3x\right]_{1}^{4} - \left[\dfrac{x^3}{3}-2x^2+7x\right]_{1}^{4}$

$= \dfrac{33}{2}-12 = \dfrac{9}{2}$

12) a) $x_0 = 0:\quad y_0 = \sqrt{9} = 3$

$x_1 = 1:\quad y_1 = \sqrt{8} = 2.8284$

$x_2 = 2:\quad y_2 = \sqrt{5} = 2.2361$

$x_3 = 3:\quad y_3 = \sqrt{0} = 0$

$h = \dfrac{(3-0)}{3} = 1$

$\int_{a}^{b}y\,dx \approx \dfrac{1}{2}[(3+0)+2(2.8284+2.2361)] = 6.5645 \approx 6.56 \text{ (to 3 s.f.)}$

b) $x_0 = 0.2:\quad y_0 = 0.2^{0.04} = 0.93765$
$x_1 = 0.4:\quad y_1 = 0.4^{0.16} = 0.86363$
$x_2 = 0.6:\quad y_2 = 0.6^{0.36} = 0.83202$
$x_3 = 0.8:\quad y_3 = 0.8^{0.64} = 0.86692$
$x_4 = 1:\quad y_4 = 1^1 = 1$
$x_5 = 1.2:\quad y_5 = 1.2^{1.44} = 1.30023$

$h = \dfrac{(1.2-0.2)}{5} = 0.2$

$\int_{a}^{b}y\,dx \approx \dfrac{0.2}{2}[0.93765+2(0.86363+0.83202+0.86692+1)+1.30023]$

$\approx 0.9363 \text{ (to 4 s.f.)}$

Index